DESTINY
DEFINING
DECISIONS

Also by Aleks George Srbinoski.

Maximum Mental Health: Overcome Depression, Anxiety and other Mental Illnesses with 20 Principles for Happier and Healthier Living

Happiness Up Stress Down: Increase Happiness and Decrease Stress in just 2 Minutes a Day over 2 Weeks and Help your Community

60 Minute Success Secrets Series Books

Motivation Now

Instant Inner Calm

10 Life Success Secrets Revealed

Precision Language

The 7 Mental Viruses Crushing Your Potential

Stay tuned for more books to be released in 2015

Books available on Amazon and through other major book distributors.

Mass copies may be directly sought from the author.

Destiny Defining Decisions

Best-Selling Entrepreneurs Reveal their Greatest Success Secrets

Aleks George Srbinoski

FULFILLING HAPPINESS PUBLISHING

Disclaimer

The author, contributors and publisher shall have neither liability nor responsibility to any person or entity with respect to any of the information, strategies or exercises contained in this document. The user assumes all risk for any injury, loss or damage caused or alleged to be caused, directly or indirectly by using any information, strategies or exercises described in the "Destiny Defining Decisions" book and related materials. All information is generalist in nature. Should any reader make use of information contained herein, this is their decision, and the contributors (and their companies), authors and publishers do not assume any responsibilities whatsoever under any circumstances or conditions.

Copyright

1st ed.
ISBN 978-0-9925826-0-9

For my father who always told me to "keep going." I will!

Acknowledgements

Thank you to all my incredible guests. Our time together was short, but the lessons offered remain timeless.

To my Dutchess, you are my true north and always the greatest source of assistance.

To the mistro James Love, thank you for being such a wonderful part of the shows that inspired this book.

To my family, thanks to you, "little Aleks" might actually be growing up!

As for all my friends and clients of the past, present and future, may the inspiration I draw from our encounters return to you tenfold.

CONTENTS

Preface: Discovering the 7 Keys to Entrepreneurial Success

Have you ever wondered what the strategies of excellence are that guide the ultra-successful? The kind of people who run multi-multi-million dollar companies, who publish New York Times Bestselling books (with some individual title's having sold more than 1 million copies on their own), and who have a combined net worth of over $300 million.

This was the question I continued to churn through my mind as I spent countless hours poring over the interview transcripts that make up this book. Through this process, I realized success does not exist in a vacuum. It is not restricted to genetically gifted geniuses and it is available to those willing to dig deep enough.

However, you must know where to dig. You need a map and expert guides; business expedition leaders with the right tools and a willingness to share them. Otherwise, your journey could end with the giant hole you dug caving in on you. My job is to help you avoid such a fate, a destiny worse than death – that of a fruitless life filled with failure and regret.

Fortunately for you dear reader, I have been able to do most of the planning. I went out and found 11 expert entrepreneurial guides, all ultra-successful individuals. Through my interviews with them, I discovered 7 key skills for success and in particular, one common theme, a universal law and essential ingredient shared amongst them all.

These 7 invaluable entrepreneurial skills are listed below in no particular order, except for the final one, which is the most important. They were all uncovered through my discussions with these amazing individuals. Throughout your journey, a range of exercises and principles to enhance your proficiency in all of these skills will be revealed. By understanding and utilizing the skills on this list, you too can become one of the next entrepreneurial MARVELS. Time now to reveal each skill.

7. Masterful Negotiation

An entrepreneur must know how to negotiate. Your ability to ethically influence others, know your worth and be treated with respect is crucial. Too many entrepreneurs struggle to assert themselves, are taken advantage of and feel lost in this area. To assist you, you are going to learn some fantastic and simple techniques from one of the most decorated negotiation teachers in the world, Professor Stuart Diamond. You will learn the 3 key rules for negotiating, how to create mutually beneficial situations in any context and I will offer the 4C's of Persuasive Communication.

6. Advanced Time Management

The ability to revolutionize the way you use your time and exponentially improve your productivity is a skill most people can only ever dream of. With so much to do and because of the endless distractions that make up the modern world, managing time is a fundamental necessity for success. Former expert in psychological warfare and motivational guru, Steve Chandler, will reveal an impressive advanced system of "non-linear" time management, and you will also learn how to best prepare yourself mentally to get maximum efficiency out of your time.

5. Resourcefulness and Possibilities Thinking

Your potential is limitless. We all have limited resources but our ability to be infinitely resourceful is not to be underestimated. Utilizing creativity, accurately projecting into the future and thinking in unconventional ways is frequently visible in highly successful entrepreneurs. In this category we draw from Randy Komisar, a very high net worth multi-organizational Silicon Valley CEO and venture capital expert. He talks about how to succeed in multiple roles and classic books connoisseur Tom Butler-Bowdon shows why age is no barrier to success. Strategies on creativity building and developing an empowering future are also offered.

4. Values and Passions Utilization

What could be more important in terms of building and maintaining success than understanding and developing your own values and passions? Finding your passions will naturally fortify your personal strengths and living by your values is the only true way to find meaningful success and happiness. In this context Tony Alessandra reveals how to create a lasting legacy, whilst Jenn Lim, CEO/Co-Founder of Delivering Happiness and business partner of Tony Hsieh (CEO of Zappos , valued at $1.2 Billion) expresses how happiness is the key to building a company worth billions as well as the secret to enhancing organizational and public communities. You will also get acquainted with a process to help you develop your deepest values and become more abundant, and a method for effectively pursuing your passions.

3. Entrepreneurial Planning

Only a fool would jump on and commit to any business idea. Creating a plan that will work is the holy grail of entrepreneurship. In this category, we draw from the experience of single mother Eve Adamson, who decided to risk all her security to become a successful freelance consultant and we pick up strategies from very high net-worth individual Richard Koch, who offers the key processes he used early in his career to build an entire organization from scratch that went on to be massively successful. In this area you will discover the three key considerations required to become successful in any new venture, how to niche a new business and find the best potential employees, and I'll reveal the how to find the best training and build a business model around your passions process.

2. Leadership Techniques

Success requires you take the lead! The person who can get their message across the most effectively is the one who will win every time. In this category, you will learn the art of powerful and precise communication from the world's leading and multi-million book selling executive coach Marshall Goldsmith, essential non-verbal influence tactics from organizational accountability expert John G. Miller, and value creation and knowledge sharing skills from the #1 best-selling business author in Australia, Andrew Griffiths.

You will also learn how to instantly read and get a feel for people, succeed in all stages of life and discover how to offer empowering feedback to enhance performance.

1. Stepping through Fear and into Freedom

This is without a shadow of a doubt, the #1 skill for entrepreneurial and life success. The issue of moving through fear was the common problem every entrepreneur faced and their step by step approach of moving through it in order to find their freedom was the solution. This category is about more than techniques, it is about developing a mindset of courage and the best way to understand how to create it is by listening to each expert's inspirational story. Once you have made your decision to step through fear and into freedom, the four P's of Accountability is also a fantastic process offered to keep you on your new life path.

Summary

Once again, below are the 7 essential skills (with the final one being the most universally important) for becoming one of the next entrepreneurial MARVELS. These fundamental attributes were discovered through hundreds of hours of study and created in order to serve the next generation of business superstars.

They are:

Masterful Negotiation

Advanced Time Management

Resourcefulness and Possibilities Thinking

Values and Passions Utilization

Entrepreneurial Planning

Leadership Techniques

Stepping Through Fear and into Freedom

Through this book, you are going to receive expert guidance and techniques in each area. These are the people you must listen to if you want to find success. All of them are best-selling authors, leaders in their field, and their combined net worth is over $300 million. Enjoy the transformative process that awaits you now.

All of the interviews to follow are transcripts of conversations broadcast as part of *The Fulfilling Happiness Edge* radio show. Each show was themed around the featured guest's expertise and several additional segments were offered to complement each interview. As a bonus for all first edition owners of this book, you will be given free download access to every single show. This will enable you to listen to the interviews, related news stories, and a range of other segments from each complete show. The shows are designed to act as brief self-development seminars.

To further aid your education and overall experience of this book, I have decided to include two of the individual learning strategies that were part of each show. Since there were 11 shows, you will be given 11 specific psychological processes to help you enhance your self-development and 11 satirical "fantasy gifts." The reason for each fantasy gift is to reveal and reinforce in a fun and unique way the truth about personal and entrepreneurial success. *In simple terms, they are to help you smile, evade charlatans, and avoid succumbing to short cuts.*

I am certain that understanding the "destiny-defining decisions" of other empowering individuals will give you the knowledge and inspiration to forge your own distinguished path. The road ahead is about to become brighter.

2 List of Experts

Happiness Movement Maverick

Jenn Lim, CEO of **Delivering Happiness**, with business partner Tony Hsieh (CEO of Zappos, valued at $1.2 Billion) runs the organization inspired by the #1 New York Times best-selling book Delivering Happiness. Although primarily authored by Tony Hsieh, Jenn also played a vital role in the creation and authorship of the book and the massive "happiness movement" that has resulted from it. An extended interview with her is offered.

Natural Negotiator

Professor Stuart Diamond, *New York Times* best-selling author of **Getting More**. *The Wall Street Journal* FINS blog called it the best book to read for your career in 2011. The Wharton School Professor and Pulitzer Prize-winning journalist has taught negotiation to over 30,000 people in 50 countries, including executives from 51 of the Global 100 companies.

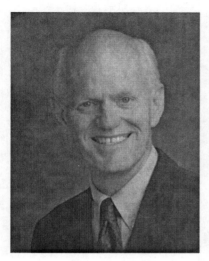

Exceptional Executive Coach

Dr Marshall Goldsmith, one of Forbes 5 most respected executive coaches and multi-million selling author of *Mojo* and *What Got You Here Won't Get You There* – a *Wall Street Journal* #1 business book, and winner of business book of the year.

Sensational Speaker

Dr. Tony Alessandra is a prolific author with 27 books translated into over 50 foreign language editions, including the newly revised, best-selling *The New Art of Managing People*. He is a graduate professor of marketing, entrepreneur, business author, and Hall of Fame keynote speaker.

Motivational Master

Steve Chandler is the best-selling author of *100 Ways to Motivate Yourself* and 30 other books that have been translated into over 25 languages. His personal success coaching, public speaking, and business consulting have been used by CEOs, top professionals, major universities, and over 30 Fortune 500 companies.

Fearless Freelancer

Eve Adamson, 5 time *New York Times* best-selling author and freelance writer who has written or co-authored over 65 books. She is an in demand *celebrity ghostwriter* and has written on self-development, psychology, stress management, Zen, cooking, holistic health, and more.

Classic Books Connoisseur

Tom Butler-Bowdon is the best-selling author of *50 Self-Help Classics*, the first guide to personal development literature. This book was followed by *50 Success Classics*, *50 Spiritual Classics*, *50 Psychology Classics*, and *50 Prosperity Classics*. The series has been published in 21 languages and is sold in over 30 countries.

Bold Business Builder

Richard Koch, new ventures investor and international best-selling author of *The 80/20 Principle*, which has sold more than a million copies and has been translated into 34 languages. His most recent title is *The 80/20 Manager*.

Acclaimed Aussie Author

Andrew Griffiths is Australia's number 1 best-selling small business author with 11 hugely successful books sold in 50 countries all over the world. His latest book, *The Me Myth*, is his first personal growth book and has won acclaim as one of the most inspirational self-improvement books ever written by an Australian author.

Passionate Persuader

John G. Miller, Organizational Personal Accountability Specialist and best-selling author of *QBQ! The Question Behind The Question, Flipping the Switch* and *Outstanding*! He also is the co-author with wife Karen of *Parenting the QBQ Way*.

Learned Leader

Randy Komisar is the author of the best-selling *The Monk and the Riddle*. He is a founding director of TiVo, was a co-founder of Claris Corporation, served as CEO for LucasArts Entertainment and Crystal Dynamics, and acted as a "virtual CEO" for such companies as WebTV and GlobalGiving.

Back from the Dead -

Special Inspirational Interview with **Anthony Catalano**

Would You Like More FREE Resources to Help You Build Your Own Unique Business?

This book offers some of the greatest lessons learnt by world-leading entrepreneurs with specialist skills across a range of disciplines.

To help you further develop the skills you need to succeed, I created the extra resources page.

It includes access to:

- **All 11 radio show/seminars on which this book is based**
- Bonus Interviews
- **A High Level Goal Setting Process**
- Cheat Sheets and Templates
- **Fast and focused self-development techniques**

And More…

Grab them all now at:
FulfillingHappiness.com/dddbonuses

Introduction – My Story and Yours

You are a fool, my friend. A beautiful, magnificent, crazy fool! Most people just don't "get it" and they don't "get you". Why would you risk it all? Your finances, your career, your health! Your family, friends and your ever-so-precious time. Time you can never get back. Hours turn into days, into weeks, into months, and into years spent in search of that personal "holy grail". The goal is so simple, but the price is enormous.

I'm going to be blunt. **Entrepreneurship is inevitable for those seeking freedom and fulfillment.** Any way you slice it, working for someone else is rarely gratifying in the long run. Of course there are a few exceptions, but truly satisfying your creative desires as an employee is as likely as finding a winning lottery ticket.

Deep down, I know why you're here and who you are. You having read this far tells me a great deal about you. As a self-development seeker and entrepreneur, you are a special breed of person. The kind of person I understand and admire and to prove it, I'll create a list of 10 things I know you want from your life.

You want to:

Take control

Find challenge

Be creative

Live life on your terms

Express yourself freely and fully

Achieve something worthwhile

Be paid well for your efforts

Grow and develop

Understand the true nature of people, business and life

Leave a meaningful legacy.

You want to be happy and fulfilled, and you know the only way to achieve this is by seeking out a new authentic path. So what's stopping you? The four letter F-word. Fear! In particular, fear of failure.

However, I want you to know something. Through this book, you are going to learn from a wonderful range of incredible best-selling entrepreneurial expert authors. Every one of them had to deal with and learn to overcome the exact same emotion.

Just like you, they've felt lost, made mistakes, and risked more than they ever wanted to. Despite the difficulties, they made it through to the other side, and now they have very generously offered to share their wisdom with you.

The best decision you have ever made

Imagine you are given an audience with a true role model. Someone you admire, respect, and love to learn from. However, there is a catch, which is that your time together is short. You only have the opportunity to ask one key question.

What will it be? I would want to discover the origin of the person's success and happiness. How did they become who they are, and how can I utilize this knowledge to better myself? As you will discover, I had the opportunity to do just that, and I will be sharing their wisdom, experience and guidance with you shortly.

I better introduce myself

Hi, I'm Aleks George Srbinoski (Aleks George for short). I'm actually an "accidental entrepreneur". My highest purpose in life is to help as many people as possible become as happy and fulfilled as they are willing to become.

Then why am I an entrepreneur, and why do I like to speak to and educate other entrepreneurs? It is because I have come to realize that entrepreneurship is the most authentic and direct path toward success and happiness.

Where do success and happiness come from?

My formal educational background was in Clinical Psychology. I was trained to assist people with what is wrong by helping them cope with stress, depression, anxiety, and so on. However, something very unexpected happened in my final year of study. I was introduced to the science of happiness. Which very much is about finding and enhancing what is "already right" in people.

This side subject soon became an exuberant passion. I wanted to know everything there was to know about happiness. Then another twist was revealed. Research demonstrated that the happiest people were also the most successful.

Along with happiness, I started to study the principles of success. Soon, I hit a major road block based on these research findings.

1. **Happiness leads to success, but success as the primary driver rarely leads to happiness.**

2. **To find happiness, you need to actively pursue your passions.**

3. **If happiness leads to success and pursuing your passions lead to happiness, then finding a career that allows you to**

fully pursue your passions would lead to the greatest success and happiness.

Fantastic! I had discovered the secret. There was only one problem: How many employees have the freedom to tailor their job to best complement their natural strengths and passions? One in 10,000 maybe. I don't actually know, but the answer is going to be tiny.

How I became an entrepreneur, and why I'm happy I did

The monk said, *"The Number 1 regret people have in their life is not taking enough leaps of faith!"*

The reality inside that statement floored me. I struggled to breathe as the realization sunk into my body. It wasn't just statistically true; a vocal arrow had struck a personal bull's-eye. My mind pulled me back to the hospital.

The ward was bleak. Always eerily quiet. A clinical world where clock ticks seemed to scream, and that vile smell attacked more than the air, the walls, and the floors. It attached itself to the people themselves as if they, too, had been harshly scrubbed down with disinfectant.

The worst part was the uncertainty. You never really knew who would survive the night. Forming relationships felt as futile as trying to build a house in hurricane season. The foundations could be swept away at any time. The morning would come and the bed would be empty. Then, in a blink of an eye, a new soul on the verge of departure would fill the space.

There was one woman in particular. Her gaze alone stripped me down to my very core. She oozed fear, regret, and sadness. Our time together was deeply confronting and undeniably life altering. The woman that changed me could barely speak English. Her condition was incurable. She seemed to have some idea of who I was but it really didn't matter.

As the young, "gung ho" clinical psychologist, part of my job was to assist on the Palliative Care ward. Naively, I thought I was ready to go in and solve the problems of the dying. Only it wasn't I who would be offering the greatest life lessons, instead, I would be receiving them.

After all, how much counselling can you give to a woman you can barely speak to? As it turned out, it wouldn't be an issue. The majority of our time together was spent in silence, holding hands, with her squeezing mine at increasingly irregular intervals.

Hand in hand, mostly in silence, we contemplated life. I wondered why her family never seemed to be around, how she had become so overweight, and why she hadn't taken the time to learn English, having been in the country for many years.

Occasionally, she would speak in her broken tongue, and almost every word was tainted with regret. She would frequently apologize about her English, speak about doing work she used to hate, family relationships that had soured, and I would listen. It really was too late to do anything about it.

I thought about the other people I worked with on the ward. It was strange. Those in the most physical pain almost always were in the greatest emotional pain and had the biggest regrets. Their language was littered with "should have", "could have", "wished I'd," "why didn't I" ...

Then there were the few patients I came across who were at peace. Despite their circumstances they would smile often, joke, and ask about me with great curiosity. Even though their bodies were on the verge of final retirement, their eyes were bright and alive.

Often surrounded by friends and family, these people would tell fascinating stories about the risks they had taken, failures learnt from and the great rewards received. Just like me, they didn't know what would happen tomorrow, but they seemed ready.

Her name was Maria. After what would be my final session with her, I actually knew I wouldn't be seeing her again. I had done my best to assist her, and I could tell she appreciated it, and yet we both knew she had not found peace.

Following the last time we spoke, I sensed she would be leaving soon, and I became very angry. I stormed out of the hospital, and with a red-hot face and clenched fists I started walking. My head was swirling with confusion.

I had no idea why I was so angry. I soon realized what it was. I hated the feeling of helplessness. I was angry at the truth. All those life clichés had punched me straight in the face. You only live once, follow your dreams, blah, blah, blah; it was all excruciatingly true.
After that day, I thought more and more about the importance of happiness and how I could do so much more for others if I quit employment and went out on my own. Maria had shaken me out of my naivety.

I had become afraid! But I was not afraid of death. Rather, I was afraid of not living. Not living fully, openly, and authentically.

Accidental entrepreneur

I became an entrepreneur not out of desire, but out of necessity. I didn't even know what the word meant until after finishing my university studies. I just wanted to be happy. However, in order to follow my heart and pursue my passions I would have to stop being an employee. I would have to quit my job.

The job I had trained for 6 years to do.

The job with the very handsome paycheck and career prospects.

The job that only a year before as a struggling student, I had so desperately wanted.

It was a terrifying decision, and I had no idea if it would be the right one.

I quit my job.

It has been a challenging road.

Overall, I have had many more failures than successes.

But I have no regrets

And ...

I am happy!

The monk said, *"The Number 1 regret people have in their life is not taking enough leaps of faith!"* I found myself back in the presence of the monk. She was a guest speaker at a happiness conference. Part of her job was to prepare people for a "good death", and not taking enough chances was clearly the greatest regret of the dying.

I started having a fantastic time. Contemplating life and death is much more enriching when you know you're on the right path. I came to realize that our decisions really do define us, both in life and all the way through to our death.

But I still needed help!

The entrepreneurial road is such a tough and lonely road. Although I had become happier overall since quitting my job, I was still very lost and confused. I needed guidance. However, I did not want to just speak to anyone, I wanted to learn from the very best. I wanted to talk to the high-level experts.

Of course the question became: how could I get them? As an unknown new entrepreneur, I couldn't just ring them up and talk to them. Or could I? Perhaps if the offer was compelling enough, then they would agree to speak to me.

I decided to build a unique entrepreneurial self-development show called *The Fulfilling Happiness Edge*. The shows would act as entertaining short seminars and feature my interviews with best-selling entrepreneurs. Furthermore, I promised the interviews would also later be turned into a book. I declared I would do almost all the work in terms of creation, promotion, and in sharing their message if they agreed to grant me a short interview. With persistence and time, enough said, "YES!" (Tip: If you want to speak to or work with an established expert in your industry, make it very easy for them to say "yes").

The Result

As previously stated, since it is fear that stops most of us from living our best life, I decided to base every interview around the same question. A question that would uncover their key moments of transformation.

"What was the thought process behind the best life-changing decision you have ever made?"

Although I had no idea this would happen, every single answer was in some way related to entrepreneurship. Their answers have been practical, enlightening, and truly inspiring. The reality is that not everyone will find success. The majority of people will succumb to their fears, and they will come to the end of their lives filled with major regrets, having wished they had taken more "leaps of faith."

Nevertheless, I am convinced that studying the mindset behind the key decisions of the trail blazers that have preceded you will offer you the best chances of success. To understand success, we must uncover its origins. Each expert's story does just that.

You will discover how:

A former commercial diver who suffered a life threatening and career-ending injury, reluctantly changed careers and went on to become Australia's #1 business author.

A world-leading master negotiator became even more of an expert by studying and interacting with his son, who he did not have until he was in his 50s.

A struggling single mother, desperate to have more time with her child, quit her job and the much sought-after security in order to forge a new career as a formidable freelancer.

A former lawyer who, after a strange, confidential encounter in a dark room, went on to become a key organizational leader across Silicon Valley and develop into a highly eclectic entrepreneur.

An ex-army officer trained in "psychological warfare" re-assembled his knowledge in order to help others and become a prolific author and world-renowned success coach.

The above examples are only a sample of the stories behind the experts you are about to meet. It's now time to have them reveal the full story.

$2,000 to Leave: Delivering Happiness CEO Discusses Profits, Positivity, and Personal Values

She is the "Happiness Movement Maverick," Jenn Lim.

Will positivity and personal values alignment with company culture lead to profits? Delivering Happiness CEO Jenn Lim (pictured left) and Zappos CEO Tony Hsieh will tell you that it does. In fact, at Zappos, a company that is valued at over 1 billion dollars, new trainees are offered $2,000 to leave if they do not feel positively aligned to the company values and culture. Delivering Happiness also follows the same procedures.

In this special extended interview conducted in March 2011, Jenn reported how the company values of Zappos were created from the input of every person on staff, and this is one of the main reasons why their staff retention, customer service, and productivity are so impressive. She also spoke candidly about how these values went on to create a sense of social capital and spawn the massive Delivering Happiness social movement and associated company.

After having already spent thousands of dollars on training people, you would only ever voluntarily pay someone $2,000 to leave your company if you truly believed that better people, greater opportunities, and higher profitability were still available to you. Your personal life follows the same principles. Assuming there are no issues around personal safety, the only reason you would ever end a personal relationship is because you believe there are greater opportunities for fun and fulfillment with someone else.

After the interview, I asked myself, "What kind of a mindset is required in order for us to connect to our deepest and most inspiring values and be willing to get rid of the people who could compromise them?" The answer lies in the difference between abundance versus scarcity based thinking. Life is filled with contrasts. Thinking styles are no different. Some are optimists, and others pessimists. Some people have an open, expressive, and abundance-focused style of thinking, but unfortunately, most people are trained to be scarcity-focused.

The question then becomes: how do you access the emotional state and mindset of abundance? After the interview you will discover a simple three-step process to assist you in opening up your mind to abundance and positive values-based thinking.

In my extended interview with Jenn, you will discover ...

- The simple four-step model that Delivering Happiness bases all their successful business and community actions on
- **The power of positive intention and how just one business idea can lead to the actual creation of better communities**
- The importance of partnering with someone you trust. Jenn speaks candidly about her relationship with Tony Hsieh and how they play the role of each other's "back-up brain"
- **Why every single employee from the ground up is involved in the creation of Delivering Happiness company and community culture**
- How to have real fun spreading your message
- **The incredible ripple effect of purpose based actions.**

Aleks: Hello, and welcome. I'm Aleks George Srbinoski, founder of **FulfillingHappiness.com** and today I'm talking to Jenn Lim from Delivering Happiness, an organization inspired by the bestselling book *Delivering Happiness* by Zappos CEO and entrepreneur Tony Hsieh. (Jenn also played a vital role in the creation and authorship of the book). *Delivering Happiness* has led to a large-scale movement involving thousands of people across the USA and the world and has been endorsed by high-profile celebrities like Ashton Kutcher and Demi Moore. Jenn is the CEO and "Chief Happiness Officer" of Delivering Happiness. First of all, how are you today, Jenn?

Jenn: I'm good Aleks, how are you?

Aleks: I'm doing really well. What I'd like to ask first, for those people who aren't familiar with Delivering Happiness, can you tell me what that book is about and what the movement is about that has come from it?

Jenn: Sure! So, *Delivering Happiness* is the book that Tony and I worked on. He wrote most of it and it's a lot of autobiographical stuff of his growing up, being a young entrepreneur, and all of the failures that he went through along the way. Most people think he's so successful and an overnight success but, in reality, there were a lot of trials and tribulations that he had to overcome in order to get to where he is today. Basically it goes through that journey but comes back to the notion of, actually more of a realization that it's not about the money or the status or the creation of a company. It's really about the happiness of yourself and the people around you, and he applied those concepts, which are based on scientific research, to his company.

If you make your employees happy then your customers are actually happy, too, and you can actually have a more profitable and successful company. So, that was the epiphany he got out of it, and now that the book has been out and has done pretty well on the bestsellers list, he just concluded a 3 ½ month tour on a tour bus across the country, 23 cities. It was less about promoting the book and more about how you can actually change your life, business, or organization based on the premises of happiness frameworks.

So, after that ended, which was December, we realized there was this community growing out of it and that's why we just announced a few weeks ago, at South by Southwest, that we're going to become a company called Delivering Happiness with our #1 goal of inspiring and spreading these models of happiness so that people on a personal or on a business level can adopt the ideas in their lives. Number one for us is the community that is organically growing out of it, and we want to be the platform they can connect to one another in pursing this decision.

Aleks: Excellent, so you're actually becoming a company as an offshoot from the actual book?

Jenn: Right, yeah. So the company, Tony and I are partners in it and we announced that I am the CEO and Chief Happiness Officer of it.

Aleks: Wonderful! Has the company actually begun or is that to begin soon?

Jenn: No, we've begun. Technically, the company started when the book was being written, but it was more so an official announcement to let people know that we are in it for the long haul. It's just creating a sustainable business basically from a financial standpoint so that we can support our great goal and higher purposes and really nurture this community that has been created out of it.

Aleks: Okay, so you talk about a higher purpose. I'm always talking about purpose, and I think it is probably the most important thing to happiness. What is the greater purpose of Delivering Happiness? What is it you are aiming to achieve?

Jenn: Like I mentioned before, it's the community. After the book came out we started hearing from people and it was not just from business folks, which was kind of expected because the book was marketed as a business book, but we started hearing from people from other sectors — from hospitals, from schools, and students; even churches and government.

So, basically there was this universal chord being strung, and as the book was translated into other languages, we started hearing from all of these different countries of very similar tales of, "Thank you for writing this book because now I'm going to change the way I do my business or the way I look at life" and it was really humbling to see that message could impact people in different ways.

Number one for us is training the community. Internally we call it ICEE, and that stands for Inspire, and we get inspired by people telling us how they've changed their lives. The C stands for Connect, so connecting the community around us. The first E stands for Education, so educating people based on the research and scientific studies done on happiness. And the last E stands for Experience. We want to provide meaningful experiences because in the end it's more about that. That equates to your greater happiness less than material goods.

Aleks: ICEE sounds fantastic! I'd like to know how did you meet Tony, and how did you end up working on this book with him?

Jenn: We've actually been friends for a long time and we met back in the day, in the late 90s, at his loft, where we had a mutual friend and we just, I don't know, had a really good connection. I think the thing that Tony and I share and what really bonds us today, is just this whole **feeling of being utterly honest and being able to say anything that we want to say to each other and without fear of judgment or anything. We actually call each other "backup brain" now because we share so many values in that sense.**

So, that happened over 11 years ago, and since then I was a freelance consultant and I worked on Zappos projects along the way so I kind of saw Zappos grow. I always considered it kind of like my best friend's little brother when you see them in grade school and all of a sudden it's a tall huge thing that you can't even recognize, but that's how I see Zappos.

I've been doing a lot of projects for them over the years, including helping them relocate to Vegas and the *Culture Book* I still work on with them today because one of my passions is writing. So when Tony got approached by publishers asking if he could write a book about his experiences, he came to me and asked me if I wanted to be a part of it.

Aleks: What exactly was your role within creating that book?

Jenn: So, I basically ... we locked ourselves in a cabin in Lake Tahoe on Labor Day in 2009 and he wrote all the segments of his in first-person, he wrote to his own voice in the book and I helped curate because we wanted to put third-party content in there, in the sense of hearing from customers and employees. So those stories I helped curate and edit and I wrote my own piece about the *Culture Book*. Basically just helped organize, put it altogether, and cracked the whip.

Aleks: Fantastic. You actually said something really interesting because obviously I am very much into happiness research from all sorts of perspectives. You're talking about being each other's "backup brain," and it's really kind of interesting when you look at the research. Mirroring runs in the brain and when we match up with each other, the same parts of the brain light up. I just have this image of you two working with each other, and if we had some sort of machine that could look into your brains it would be matched up and dancing, which is a pretty cool image to have in mind.

I wanted to know a little about the culture of Zappos. Can you explain to me what the big focus is with the culture of Zappos? How do you do things differently than how other organizations have?

Jenn: Sure, it was sort of an **evolution of how culture became number one at Zappos. First, it being an online retailer of shoes, then it became customer service being number one, then it became culture in terms of treating your employees well.**

So that was the basic notion and being able to scale that in a way that as your company grows that the culture doesn't get out of hand — the way Zappos did it, they implemented 10 Core Values.

So about six years ago it started, and basically they surveyed the company, what the core values would be from a personal and corporate level and it actually took a while.

It took a year to narrow it down to **10 Core Values and that's what they live and die by, it's what they hire and fire by and if you don't live up to these core values it doesn't matter if you're a rock star engineer or lawyer, you wouldn't work at Zappos if you didn't believe in those values.**

Aleks: Right, because it's about the harmony and the long-term vision.

Jenn: Yeah, for sure. Because that's the only way to make it scalable.

Aleks: Okay, so with these values ... did you actually get the whole organization involved in the creation of the values?

Jenn: That's right, and that's why it took a long time to do because it was the surveys of all the employees at that time of what values they would believe in to nominate for the corporate core values.

Aleks: Okay. But then that also gets everyone involved so they all take ownership in that process.

Jenn: Exactly, and that's also what's important in the sense that there are a lot of companies with core values but it was pretty much conceived by senior management level, senior level meetings, and you know, put on a plaque in the lunchroom wall or something that doesn't really have meaning to it.

The people didn't really create it themselves, and that was part of the process and idea behind making people feel that they're a part of it and they should own it instead of just believe in it.

Aleks: Wonderful! So I want to move on to the bus. I want to know about the bus, what's involved in these bus tours, and what is the purpose of them?

Jenn: All right, so it's all pretty organic because the bus idea originally came from South by Southwest a year ago and the book had not been launched yet, it hadn't come out and we knew a good place to start would be talking to people about the book. We were going to throw a party but at that time it was 10 days before South By started and everything was either full or just really expensive.

Instead we asked ourselves, "Why don't we rent a bus?" and we branded it Delivering Happiness, wrapped it, hired a full time bartender, got a balloon artist on board, and we just took it on the road.

It ended up being the place that everyone wanted to be because you didn't have to wait in line, you could get drinks, and it would take you to wherever you wanted to go. So, it was that idea that spun into when people started asking us what are you going to do for the book tour and people were like, you know, I guess the traditional way of doing book tours of going to cities and doing signings didn't sound exciting so we decided to do the next iteration of the bus. So we actually bought a bus from the Dave Matthews Band base player (apparently they're doing pretty well if the base player has his own bus) and we did a quick makeover and made it a little happier and took it on the road.

We had about 10 people on the road at any given time and in 3 ½ months, 23 cities. **The whole purpose behind it was not about selling books, it was more about this message, and we did visits to entrepreneurs and businesses, but we also went to hospitals and schools.** We went to Times Square and did a Times Square ambush of books and T-shirts and this whole notion of there's no real reason or no ulterior motive of what we're doing, we just want to spread this message of delivering happiness.

Aleks: Sure, and then by doing that the effect is that it is branding. Everything we do in a way is branding, and if you're just being genuine and kind and delivering happiness in every possible scenario you can think of, well then what better spotlight of what you guys are about then that?

Jenn: Yeah, I guess for us from an experience standpoint it was probably one of the most exhausting times of our lives, just being on that bus, but it was amazing because we were able to talk to people that emailed us and got to meet them in person. Again, it goes back to what I was saying earlier, the ICEE, it's the experiences and the fact that we were being able to provide experiences for people that they wouldn't have otherwise.

That meant the most to us, and that's why the theme of the tour was "Inspire or Be Inspired" because with every story or person that we met that was inspired to do something different in their lives because of it, that's basically inspiring us to do what we're doing today and why we're launching a company around it.

Aleks: Have you got one in mind? You're talking about people being inspired by the tour and what you guys have been doing – does someone in particular come to mind that meant something to you?

Jenn: Wow, there's just so many, but depending on from a business standpoint or non-business standpoint but someone had said he was on the brink of committing suicide and because he read the book it gave him some hope that things would change. So, it went from that level to a mom writing to us saying, "I want to be the CMP of the household, meaning the Chief Managing Parent and instilling core values and culture in my family because I'm a good mom but I know I can be better" and that's another level. Then, there are the students that get so much out of it.

For example, I told my story at the University of Iowa because they have *Delivering Happiness* as required reading in their class now, and a student asked how I got to where I am today and I basically told him that I was pre-scripted to do certain things and [was taught that] once I ended up getting into a good school to be a doctor or lawyer and learn as many instruments as I can growing up and that would equate to success. But I realized that after I started studying that it wasn't for me, so I dropped that pre-med major and I decided to pursue something I was really passionate for, which was Asian-American studies. And that's really hard for immigrant parents to digest because they work really hard and sacrifice a lot, and they didn't really want to see their kid struggling with a Bachelor in Arts; my mom wanted to see me as a doctor or lawyer.

But, I did it anyway and graduated, and lucky for me I was a product of the internet generation and became an internet consultant and five years later I got laid off. As everyone knows, the bottom fell out and that's when I realized that everything that had meant something, I thought, like the money, status, and title meant nothing at all. In the book, if you read it, that's the point where Tony and I were climbing Mount Kilimanjaro and he was actually dealing with really big life decisions as well because everyone was telling him to not bet his own bank, but to liquidate and sell Zappos rather than keep it alive, and he chose to do it anyway, and I was deciding what to do for the rest of my life.

That was when I realized it was more about doing things that were meaningful for me on a day-to-day basis and that's when I started doing my creative writing, started pursing graphic design, and freelancing around it. So fast forward years later here as CEO and I told this story in that class and a week later a student wrote to us and said, "Thank you for telling me that story because I dropped out of my pre-med major and I'm going to pursue art and education." So, that was at the beginning of the tour and that's when I started realizing that we are affecting lives in some small way or a big way, but you never know how you are going to affect other people until you put yourself out there and just do what you believe in.

Aleks: Fantastic, I think that choosing your own path is so important. I think every successful person, and happy person I've ever come across, it's always about choosing your own path.

There has to come a point where you have to let go of what everyone else expects of you — still be kind and courteous — but just decide, "no," I need to find my own personal fulfillment and meaning.

Jenn: Yeah, I think that's precisely it and I think that **it's #1 just being true to yourself, and I think that's what Tony and I have shared in our choices along the way.** In hindsight, living really parallel lives because of that decision to be real and do things that are meaningful to us, and that's what carries on to what you're passionate about, and carries on to knowing your higher purpose and knowing your real meaning in life.

Aleks: Yeah, and I guess it works out in the end. I have read the book and Tony had made some really large decisions, as well. He was in a very safe and secure, highly profitable position (I think it was with Microsoft) and then he decided I just can't do this. It's just not fulfilling, and it's just going to make me miserable. I think he was kind of miserable for a little while there.

Jenn: Yeah, he was ...

Aleks: ...and it wasn't until he made that decision to give up all that security and a lot of money to find out who I'm about, and it sounds like you've gone through a very similar process and you've even actually gone through it together many times, which is just a really wonderful thing to hear.

Jenn: Yeah, it's actually kind of funny because we were almost as parallel but as opposites on the spectrum because he had just made a lot of money through a sale to Microsoft and I was in the opposite end because I had just gotten laid off and had everything taken away from me, but we were both pondering the same question at the same time.

Aleks: Okay. So I'd like to ask you an important question now and that question is, "what was the thought process behind the best life-changing decision you've have ever made?"

Jenn: Well, like I said, I actually talked to you about it a little bit already, but **what I thought was the worst time of my life and my biggest failure was getting laid off, and in hindsight now it was probably the best thing that could have happened to me because it forced me to answer the question that I was avoiding for a long time, which was what would I do if I didn't fear the risk of failure and so after having everything taken away from me, then I decided I need to ask myself and be true to that. So, it wasn't overnight, but it was a process of just doing things based on that notion and re-prioritizing things in my life.** Then after that point I knew that if I made the decision based on what's most meaningful to me rather than money, status, career, and title, I realized the number one thing for me are the people in my life and relationships that I have. So, if I base every decision on that then I can't go wrong.

That's when I started just doing things that I actually enjoyed from a day-to-day basis, knowing that everything could be taken away at any given moment. So I guess those decisions of I'm going to start writing, I'm going to start graphic design, and I'm going to start being a freelancer because I don't see myself working for someone again, and that's where I am today.

Aleks: Okay, and you said something really important there, kind of as a subset of that question, which is, "What would I do if I wasn't afraid of failure?"

And I think that's a question that not many people ask themselves and honestly answer and do something about. Do you think that if you weren't laid off you would have still come to that decision, or do you think you may not have?

Jenn: That's interesting, I think that being laid off kind of forced it upon me faster than otherwise. But I knew that I wasn't happy. I knew that it was such an ephemeral feeling of the highlife, but from a fundamental level it didn't really touch me in ways that were meaningful because this is all parallel with things that were happening on a personal level in a sense of one of my greatest fears was losing a loved one, and I was about to lose my father. When you're faced with those kinds of things then you, well I really dug deep and asked myself how will I choose to live my life given the fact that things can change any second?

Aleks: Okay and I assume that you did lose that loved one, since then?

Jenn: Yes.

Aleks: After deciding to make that choice in how to live your life and obviously losing a loved one, which is always a shock to anyone, how did that choice help you through that process which would have been quite difficult?

Jenn: Because if I wasn't living by what I really believe in, I think everything that my loved one, my dad, would be for naught. Everything that he taught and instilled in me as values, and going back to core values of who we are as human beings, I think would have been a disrespect to all that he did for me. **So, that, along with seeing someone pass away that really is just a light in the world and having that diminish, made me even more passionate about this is our life that we need to live and be open and honest about and not be afraid to say "I love you" and not be afraid to smile at a stranger just because those things create better goodness in the world. Why dwell on things in the world or worry about things you can't control rather than control the things that you can and do the best we can?**

Aleks: What's the future for your role and for delivering happiness as a movement? What are you aiming toward?

Jenn: Again, for us, what we see, we are not basing on traditional metrics for the company, about profits, bottom line, and margins. Those things are important for creating a sustainable business but for us it's the community and the breadth and the number and meaning of interactions that we can create in the world. So everything in terms of building the revenue streams and consulting, we're going to have a lifestyle store that is similar to the brand "life is good" of inspiring merchandise, and down the line we're going to be stocking the store with experiences because we want people to have meaningful experiences in life that you'll remember, not the products or stuff that you buy.

So those are all just means to support the people, and we get inspired when we hear about people changing their lives or wanting help to change their company or organization and we're here to support that.

Aleks: So, this is a bit of an interesting question but it's almost like surreal, right. Can you believe you are doing what you are doing now?

Jenn: No, I mean that's why I always laugh when people say what do you see yourself doing in one, two or five years, and I was never really able to answer that because there was no way up until a year ago that I could have told you I would be running a company like Delivering Happiness. But it just feels so right, I just think that for both Tony and I, our paths are to be doing this right now and just being able to share what we think we can create and creating this platform of people to be united by the same vision and happiness. It's an incredible feeling.

Aleks: Sounds fantastic. So where can people find out more about Delivering Happiness?

Jenn: We have our website, it's **DeliveringHappiness.com** and we have our Facebook page which is **http://www.facebook.com/deliveringhappiness** and our biggest growth of community, a lot of interaction there. And we actually have a, we're calling it a "town hall founders community" of people that want to take it on their own to actually create town halls wherever they are in the world, and talk about how they can basically apply these frameworks of happiness to their lives and organizations, and that's been really inspiring as well.

Aleks: Excellent, we'll I share very similar ideals and values as you guys and I'm always looking for role models and I think you guys are two wonderful people, Tony and yourself and so I've had a great time speaking to you, and I wish you all the best, and I can't wait to find out what you guys are up to in the future.

Jenn: Thanks Aleks, it was nice talking to you, too.

Aleks: Thank you.

Develop Deeper Values and Greater Abundance
Focus Procedure

1. Shift your physiology

Sit tall with your shoulders back, have your head up, eyes forward and begin breathing deeply. Spend 20-60 seconds just focusing on your breathing and imagine simply letting go of all of your thoughts.

2. Find a relevant memory

With a clear mind, choose a memory where you were feeling and acting in a confident, successful and abundance/opportunity-focused way. If you can't think of such a time, imagine how you would be feeling and acting if you were confident, successful, and abundance/opportunity-focused.

3. Ask empowering questions

Maintaining your physiology and keeping those images in mind, ask yourself empowering abundance focused questions. Here are five for you to write down your answers to:

What is it that I stand for?

How do I want people to know and describe me?

What am I going to create and give?

Who shares and supports my values and would brainstorm ideas with me?

What do I need to do right now, and continue doing in the future to start turning these ideas into reality?

The only thing to do now, of course, is to put your answers into action. The first two steps of the above process can be done in a couple of minutes or less, and will easily lead you into the third step of asking empowering questions. This exercise should be practiced regularly in order to keep you aligned with your deeper values and develop your abundance focus.

Living by your own values is essential for true personal and professional success. Fortunately, you will not need to pay those who do not share your values to leave your presence. The more attuned you are to your own values and sense of abundance, the more likely it is that you will naturally gravitate toward people who share similar styles of thinking and feeling.

Fantasy Gift – X-Box Engage

In this high tech digital world of ours, speaking to others can be a real drag. Conversation and connection are becoming lost arts. Why would you ever want to talk to anyone these days when there is so much more action in the digital world?

Well, it's time to bring the old world back into the new. You're about to discover how to play the new game and take control of your reality.

Introducing …

THE BRAND NEW – "X-Box Engage … "

That's right, the new X-Box Engage takes virtual reality training to a whole new level …

– By combining virtual reality – with – wait for it … REALITY!

That's right, this imaginary machine that fits right in your pocket, in the palm of your hand, or even behind your ear allows you to feel other people's emotions just by looking at them and speaking to them.

And you won't have to consciously work on anything. Just place the virtual microscopic electrodes on your face and you will instantly be able to smile, make eye contact, and appear deeply interested and engaging without any effort at all.

Thereby creating an abundant flow of synchronised "mirror neurons" between you and anyone else you interact with, thus …

Allowing you to fully ENGAGE them within a new paradigm of virtual reality – also called reality.

And every fan of this book – will be going home with their very own X-Box Engage. Just look under your chair, it's right there … congratulations.

The X-Box Engage: The next big leap in human connection.

Form Superior Negotiation Skills and Communication Techniques by Removing "Power" from Persuasion

With the "Natural Negotiator," Professor Stuart Diamond.

Collaborative communication techniques are the backbone of superior negotiation skills. In the art of persuasion, power and force were once considered to be standard practice.

However, the use of power is a very poor method of persuasion, as I discovered in my recent interview with Stuart Diamond (pictured left). A Wharton Business School professor, best-selling author and Pulitzer Prize-winner who has taught negotiation to over 30,000 people in 50 countries, he reported how power hardly ever works at any level of negotiation.

Whether it's with children, friends, spouses, business, or politics, attempting to assert power over someone virtually always leads to resistance to you and your message. Instead of using power and logic, a much better approach is to seek collaboration by understanding the other person's perceptions and emotions and using that knowledge to move toward a situation that meets both parties' needs.

As important as those factors are, it is also crucial that you are comfortable with your own perceptions and emotions before entering into a negotiation. To find out how you can best prepare yourself psychologically for a negotiation, I created the four C's of persuasive communication to be revealed after the interview.

In my interview with Stuart Diamond, you're going to discover ...

- The three key rules for negotiating anything with anyone
- **The importance of understanding the perceptions and emotions of others**
- Battle of the sexes: find out — who are the better negotiators?
- **How to create mutually beneficial situations in any context**
- Why power and force are unnecessary in skillful negotiation and what you do need to promote instead.

Aleks: Hello, and welcome. I'm Aleks George Srbinoski, founder of **FulfillingHappiness.com** and today my guest is Professor Stuart Diamond, Pulitzer Prize-winning journalist formerly for the *New York Times* and author of the *New York Times* best-selling *Getting More*, which the *Wall Street Journal* FINS blog called "The best book to read for Your Career" in 2011. Professor Diamond is a Harvard-trained attorney and former Associate Director of the Harvard Negotiation Project. He currently is the professor of the most popular course at The Wharton School and has been so for the last 15 years.

An expert negotiation teacher and facilitator, he has worked as a consultant for the United Nations on numerous occasions and has taught negotiation to over 30,000 people in more than 50 countries, including executives from 51 of the Global 100 companies and 124 of the Global 500 including IBM, Google, Microsoft, JP Morgan, Exxon, Honda, Hewlett Packard, and many more.

To be honest, I could spend the entire interview going through Professor Diamond's list of incredible achievements, but then people wouldn't be able to learn about the decisions that have shaped his success. So let's get straight into it. Welcome, Professor Diamond.

Stuart: Thank you, glad to be here.

Aleks: Wonderful, so let's not waste any time. The question I have for you is: what was the thought process behind the best life-changing decision you have ever made?

Stuart: The best decision I have ever made in my life was to have a child. My child is Alexander, now 12 years old. I had him when I was 53 and my wife was 46, both of us were toward the end of our careers after business school and law school, etc. While I couldn't have predicted all of the ramifications of this in a business sense, I can say a number of things that were very important to me in terms of becoming much better at what I did even though I was accomplished before.

The first thing is, in having a child I learned to pay a lot more attention to the sensibilities of other people in business and in life. If you've got a defenseless thing in front of you and in order for you to be able to take care of that person, the best thing to do is to think about who they are, what they want, etc. And this actually went over to my business life.

The second thing is, he was for a long time of course unable to communicate very well with me, and so I was constantly thinking about what his perceptions were and what he was communicating, and finding better and more importantly, clearer ways to communicate with him.

The third things were management and leadership. In order to motivate him to do things – if you threaten them, if you use your power over a child, the child gets resentful and retaliates. One of the things that's been interesting to me is that over the last 10 or 12 years to put the theory together behind life, and my negotiating book *Getting More* is that **I've found that my negotiations with my child were very helpful because kids are pretty unvarnished in terms of how they perceive the world. With adults, a lot of stuff is hidden, but it is still there and my book says that perceptions and emotions are the pictures in the other person's head, and, as it were, are much more important than power, leverage, threats, walking out, rationality, and all those things that pass for negotiation theory historically but don't work very well.**

So, I negotiate with my kid all the time and I find the lessons are perfectly suitable to carry on to business, as well as people are astonished as to how successful I have been with my kid and how the same tools work in business.

Aleks: I think that's wonderful and also creates a little bit of hope for parents that they're not always doing a bad job. It's tough to raise kids well and to find the right negotiating strategy with them.

Stuart: Right, I don't ever assert power over my child. What I do is, for example, is I tell him he can have Legos or a toy on Saturday if he cleans his room all week, then if the room isn't clean on Saturday, **I don't say, "If you don't clean your room you're not getting Legos or you're not getting Legos because you haven't cleaned your room." I say, "I want nothing better than to buy you Legos today – help me buy you Legos" and that is a non-threatening situation that makes it a common problem, and it is exactly translatable to dealing with employees and partners in business. Instead of threatening people, you instead say, "How do we solve our common problem?"**

Aleks: Sure, exactly. So you've mentioned it in a few steps, but can you think of some specific examples where you would have negotiated one way before having a child and you changed the way you negotiated since having a child?

Stuart: Yes, I've become a lot more ... first of all I try to not to threaten anybody. It just doesn't work and you retaliate.

Second, if you do and you exert your power over people, they tend not to like it. So, I'm continually trying to figure out ways to give my kid power. How do I get them to make decisions or to participate in decisions?

You want to pick a restaurant, your room can be a little dirty, and you can go to bed a little later. **I don't tend to sweat the small stuff, and if you tend to do that with people in the real world, people tend to give you stuff back for it.**

You treat salespeople better and they give you a discount. You treat employees better and they stay later or put in overtime and don't to charge you. You set up a bargain — I'd like to meet your needs, I need mine met, of course, but I'd like to meet yours and that's exactly ... I certainly knew this stuff before I had a child but it's much more applicable when you're dealing with somebody who has no overlay that you get with adulthood of caution, of playing games, someone that's really unvarnished and uncensored, etc. It really gives you a sense if you focus, how exactly you use these tools in the real world.

Aleks: Okay ...

Stuart: People can learn a lot from their kids. **Kids are much more sensitive than adults about what's going on around them because they have less power. When we have less power, we become much more sensitive to what other people can do to you. So that's why women and children are better negotiators then men.**

Aleks: Hmm ...

Stuart: Children tend to lose "that power" when they get to be older they get "raw power."

Aleks: Would you say that if you can become a great negotiator with a child then you can become a great negotiator with adults?
Stuart: I would say that's true but that has to include training. For example, **women are instinctively better negotiators than men but they usually have less raw power. But women generally, if I can stereotype here, have less training than men in business negotiating, at least, because they have not been as much in the workforce or have not been trained as much.**

So if you train women effectively in negotiation then they will often wind up being better negotiators then men.

They haven't had access to the kind of tools men have had in negotiating. So instinctively women are better negotiators but not in terms of results because they have not had the training. A lot of people I talk to these days in terms of training and negotiations are women. I talk to women at eBay, women on Wall Street on learning the structure that for men has been endemic since they were first starting out in business.

Aleks: What would be just a couple of your top tips to negotiating for a beginner?

Stuart: Sure, these come from children and adults. One is **finding out the pictures in the head of the other side; it the most important thing you can do. Their perceptions and emotions, because if you don't do that, you don't even have a place to start and you don't know how to persuade them.** You shouldn't just come with your proposal and propose it. It might not even be the right proposal – that's number one.

Second, you want to **be a lot more incremental if you're having a problem.** We live in a world that is full of risk. Children do it by saying, "Can I have a cookie?", "Well, can I have a half a cookie?" "Well, can I have a quarter of a cookie?". And so with kids you say, "Well, you won't clean your room, but will you a do a quarter of your room; will you go to bed a little bit earlier?" **With people in business, you won't do the whole proposal. Would you do a trial, would you try it for a month? So being incremental is one of the hardest things for adults to learn. I think there would be a less controversial health care plan in the U.S. and peace in the Middle East, had they started 30 years ago with one clinic or one factory and scaled it up like the technology industry does.**

But most of the time there is too much, too many constituencies too fast, too many issues. I tend to want to **break it down and that's the third thing I want to do in helping them. I also want to think about what are the standards or the criteria we should use to decide. I don't want to just haggle over things. I want to know is there a fair process or fair principle we can put in place that we might both subscribe to.**

For example, innocent people shouldn't be victimized as is the case of the U.S. budget battle and perhaps putting 800,000 government employees out of work while there isn't any budget for the government. What a consumer company has said it promises consumers ... so if you're treated badly, you can say to them, "How come you're treating me badly, you are supposed to treat me well." How do I get a raise at work, what are your criteria by which you give raises and how can I meet them? So that's also very important in fashioning much better negotiation.

Aleks: Okay, that's brilliant. That really explains all of it in that sense. I thank you very much for that. So, where can people find more about you and your work?

Stuart: Sure, I have a website called **www.GettingMore.com**. The book, *Getting More* is for sale on our website, in stores and on the internet, such as Amazon. Basically, it is a very different, much more effective way of interacting with others. It includes everything from getting a job, to dealing with kids, to dealing with international politics, to traveling, to relationships, and so forth. It is told through the stories of 400 people I have taught among the 30,000 people I've taught in 50 countries and it is intended to be used immediately by anybody who sees it. The average executive makes a million dollars the first year from the book and the average individual makes $10,000 in the first six months.

Aleks: Wow! Okay. Thank you very much for being a part of this series.

Stuart: Sure, anytime, and good luck to you.

The 4 Cs of Persuasive Communication

The 4 Cs are...

Clarity

Consistency

Congruence

Commitment

Clarity

First, you want to be crystal clear about the outcome you want to have and how you are going to go about getting it. Depending on the situation, you want to have done your preparation if appropriate and be clear on what your message is about and how to cater it to the situation. The more clear you are on what you want to present and how, the more decisively you will be able to speak about what you have to offer. By having greater clarity, you will also be able to easily adapt your message to make it a mutually beneficial for everyone involved.

Consistency

Second is consistency. Because you are clear on what you want, and open to what they want, this part of the process is about continually generating benefits for working together. The more often you present benefits that will serve the needs of the other person (as well as your own), the more valid your message will become to them.

Congruence

Next is congruence. As you continue to find benefits, at the same time, you should be looking at which benefits in particular they seem to resonate with. What ideas and possibilities are they most passionate about? This is going to lead to revealing what the person's values are. Just as your message should be fully aligned and congruent with your values, you will also start to discover their values, too. The more you can align your message or offer to their values, the more persuasive you will become.

Commitment

Last is commitment. You need to be fully committed to what you are presenting. You need to be prepared for any possible objections or changes that may need to be made. You have to believe that what you have to offer is of great value, and be politely tenacious in your discussions.

If your offer is aligned with your greater purpose, and you can see how it could also be aligned to their greater purpose, this will help you remain committed to the creation of a mutually beneficial outcome.

Use the 4 Cs as a guide to get you prepared before a negotiation and as signposts during discussions. Always remember to focus on collaboration through the understanding of another person's emotions and perceptions, rather than trying to force your point of view through logic, threats, leverage, and other power plays.

Fantasy Gift – Persuasion

Imagine …

Walking into a room and "owning it."

All eyes on YOU. Ears perked, everyone open, willing and desperate to hear from you.

They want your message, they want to be transformed by your words, they want to get …

Up close and personal.

WHY?

Because they want to smell you.

Introducing "Persuasion," our newest fragrance. Just one spray and you will have instant clarity, consistency, congruence, and a deep level of commitment.

It will filter into your mind and allow you to walk the walk of someone with great finesse, presence and purpose.

People will listen to what you have to say – no matter how Pepe Le Pew your message used to be, from now on – you're going to be the Pepe Le Pow Wow of the party.

Persuasion – get yours today. You know that deep down, that's what you really want.

And every fan of this book will be going home with their very own bottle. Just look under your chair, it's right there … congratulations.

The smell of success is on you.

Do You Believe in Sharing?

This book is about making decisions that change lives. Living in a world with so much negativity, criticism and rejection, I believe every author in this book has a story that others should hear.

Destiny Defining Decisions was not easy to create and it certainly has not been a smooth process in terms of getting the message out about it. The life of a "solo entrepreneur" can be harsh and finding supportive and likeminded people is essential. We don't have large marketing budgets, major publishing contacts, PR teams or established bookselling contracts.

What we do have is a lot of hours behind a computer and a dream. What I value and rely on most, is one very special relationship and that is the one I have with you, my reader.

I have a small but important favor to ask. Can you tell others about the project?

You could mention it to your colleagues, friends and family and of course visit my site and use your social media networks to let others know as well. If possible, leaving a review at the place you obtained the book (e.g. Amazon.com) would be great as well. Whatever you decide, thank you in advance for reading this far and may you use what you have learnt to forge a greater destiny.

P.S. As a thank you, I'm sending you my next Fantasy Gift Prototype – The Share and Care Chair. You simply sit on it and instantly become the center of attention. Guaranteed to get everyone to hang off every word you say and immediately act on all the positive life changing things you tell them to do. It really is the chair where you share and show how you care. It's in the imaginary post as we speak.

When they get the book, they too will get the extra goodies at: FulfillingHappiness.com/dddbonuses

Master Executive Coach Reveals his 360-Degree Feedback Methods used to Create Successful Leaders

The "Exceptional Executive Coach" in question is Marshall Goldsmith.

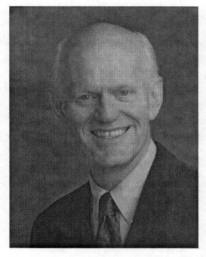

According to Master Executive Coach Marshall Goldsmith (pictured left), 360-degree feedback is essential for developing successful leaders. The highly respected multi-million selling book of the year winner stated in my interview with him that he only works with people who are completely open to receiving real feedback from every possible source of relevance.

He then uses the information gathered to tailor positive, simple, focused, and fast professional development solutions for his high-level clients. Often people are confused about how to give feedback. Most would agree that offering positive feedback is important, but an easy-to-administer process is often missing.

Through my consulting work, clients often have working relationship challenges and would frequently request simple ways to offer feedback when coaching, mentoring or assisting others. Through those experiences I developed a simple five-step "Positive Appraisal Process" to be given after the interview.

In my interview with Marshall, you're going to discover ...

- His extremely simple and highly powerful coaching philosophy
- **How to use the input of others to bring out the best in your clients and yourself**
- Why he rejects many very high-paying client offers
- **Ways to inspire others to seek and enjoy career-enhancing feedback processes**
- Why positive, simple, focused, and fast strategies are the key to coaching high-level people.

Aleks: Hello, and welcome. I'm Aleks George Srbinoski, founder of **FulfillingHappiness.com** and today my guest is Dr. Marshall Goldsmith, who has recently been recognized as one of the 15 most influential business thinkers in the world in a global bi-annual study sponsored by *The London Times*. Other acknowledgments include: American Management Association – top 50 thinkers and leaders who have influenced the field of management over the past 80 years; Institute for Management Studies – lifetime achievement award (one of two ever awarded); *Wall Street Journal* – top 10 executive educators; *Forbes* – 5 most-respected executive coaches; *Economic Times* (India) – top CEO coaches of America; and quoted by *Fast Company* as America's preeminent executive coach.

Marshall is one of a select few executive advisers who have been asked to work with over 120 major CEOs and their management teams. He is the million-selling author of numerous books, including *New York Times* best-sellers *MOJO* and *What Got You Here Won't Get You There* – a *Wall Street Journal* #1 business book and winner of the Harold Longman Award for business book of the year.

I know I've been positively influenced by his coaching philosophies, and it's a real privilege to have him with me today. Welcome, Marshall.

Marshall: Thank you very much!

Aleks: Wonderful! So basically I've got one question for you, and I think this is going to help people really understand how you became who you are in many ways. So, the question I have is, what was the thought process behind the best life-changing decision you have ever made?

Marshall: Well, mine was advice that was given to me by a gentleman named Dr. Fred Case who was my dissertation adviser. I was working down in the LA City Planning Department and I was the typical young PhD student, self-righteous know-it-all, thought I was better than everyone else, and he was getting feedback that I was coming across as somewhat angry and sort of negative and self-righteous and overly critical. So he called me in and he said I am getting this negative feedback and asked me what's going on?

So I go into this incredible monologue of the LA City Government and how screwed up it is and he looked at me and he had been working there for years and said, "Oh my goodness, Marshall Goldsmith, what a brilliant man, you have discovered the LA City Government is illogical and irrational." He said, "Marshall, I hate to tell you this but I've been working down there 20 years, and I'm incredibly slow, but I may have even figured that out myself." Then he said, "I hate to tell you, you're probably not going to get a PhD for this level of insight. Do you have any other issues?"

I go into this tirade about petty corruption. He looked at me and said, "Well, Marshall, another brilliant breakthrough for you. You have realized that when people donate millions of dollars to politicians, the politicians are nicer to those people than the people who donate to their opponents." He said, "My goodness, another brilliant insight. I don't know if you know this, but the guy pumping gas down at the corner knew all of this stuff years ago."

He looked at me and said, "You know Marshall, you're coming across as a negative, whiny, judgmental pain in the butt and this is not particularly pleasant and I'm getting negative feedback. So I'm going to give you two options. Option A, continue down this unpleasant path, and you're going to be fired from your job, and you're never going to graduate, and you won't get a PhD, and you've wasted the last four years of your life.

Option B, you can start having some fun. Life is short. Quit getting overly broad about stuff that everyone in the world knows is going on anyway." So he looked at me, he was a very wise man and he said, "what's it going to be, son?"

I said, "Dr. Case, let's have some fun here."

Well, that advice was probably the best advice I'd ever got in my life. **After *that I actually realized that number one, nobody made me God. Number two, life is inherently* irrational, which at some level I knew anyway, and number three we're all going to be equally dead so let's just have some fun here. After I came to this realization, not only did I have more fun, I made more positive difference in the world. Rather than trying to judge everyone around me, I decided I'd be better off helping them. Rather than being self-righteous or acting better than everyone, I thought maybe I would just try to understand them the best I could.** So, I'd have to say that was probably the best life-changing decision I had ever made.

Aleks: So, how did that spiral into the work you ended up doing from that point in time? I mean, obviously you've written some amazing books and *What Got You Here Won't Get You There* feeds into that philosophy you are talking about in many ways.

Marshall: Well, what it does is I am a Buddhist and this turned out to be very Buddhist philosophy. Actually, even before I became a Buddhist this was great Buddhist philosophy. The essence of Buddhism is: be happy and content now, or at least my branch of Buddhism. I use Buddhism throughout my coaching. For example, one of the elements of coaching I use is something I call "feed forward" which is a central tenet of my coaching philosophy.

In [the concept of] feedforward, Buddha said, "Only do what I teach you if it works for you. If it doesn't work for you, don't do it." Well, the way I teach feedforward: you ask for input, you take the ideas as a gift. If it works for you, use it, but if it doesn't work for you don't use it, but you don't judge or critique people who gave you ideas. You learn to shut up and say "thank you." You use what you can use, and if you don't use it you still say, "thank you" and are grateful.

It is amazing how this simple concept has changed my coaching philosophy and it's really the center of how I work with my clients. In my coaching process I don't get paid until my clients get better. I don't get paid one cent during the entire process. And "better" is not judged by me or them; it is judged by everyone around them. **I never argue with my clients. Everything is either required and they have to get feedback and talk to people about what they learn, follow up, get measured, and some other basic steps, and there's no use in arguing about that. If they don't want to do that, I just don't work with them.** I don't judge them, I just say, "No I'm just not going to work with you." Then, everything else is optional. I say take the advice I give you and the advice you learn from everyone around you, and you learn to sit there, shut up, think about it, and it has to come from your heart. If you're going to do it anyway, you have to believe in it. And that one concept, feedforward, is really the essence of how I coach people.

Aleks: Okay, great! So, what advice would you give to someone in that position who wants to be more influential at work? Obviously, you've talked about feedforward, but you have a whole bunch of habits that you've talked about before that people fall into and, shall we say, *interfere* with good relationships. What advice would you give to people as some basic tips for how to be more influential at work and be more positive at work?

Marshall: Well, **number one, I teach people to learn and ask for input. Ask a question, how can I get better? How can I be a better boss, but also a better parent, better friend, better family member? How can I be better is a question we don't ask enough. Then, listen in a nonjudgmental way, and again treat the input as a gift. Don't put people down for telling you the truth. Focus on the future, not the past.** So ask, listen, think about what people have learned, and fight the immediate urge to make excuses, get defensive, or punish the messenger. Thank people when they give you input as opposed to punishing them, and then respond.

I teach people to respond to something called "360-degree feedback" in a very positive way. Something like, **"Thank you very much for participating in this process. Overall I'm very grateful for the opportunity, and I know your time is valuable, and thank you for helping me."**

A lot of my feedback is very positive, and I teach someone to go through what the positives are and express gratitude. Then, pick one or two simple areas to improve and say, "Here's something I'd like to do better." Apologize for previous mistakes that we've made, and ask for input about how you can get even better in the future. Then, involve the other people in change. **The key to everything I teach is follow-up. I wrote an article with my friend Howard Morgan called *Leadership is a Contact Sport*, 86,000 participants in eight major corporations, and the article is really clear. The leaders that do what we teach, ask for the input, listen, respond in a positive way, follow up and get better. Leaders that don't, don't.**

Aleks: ... and it sounds so simple, and yet it's basically how we do it.

Marshall: Right, everything I do is very simple.

Aleks: Yeah, and I think that's what brings out the elegance in what you do. You've obviously been credited in many different ways. It's really broken down into some very simple philosophies, and I guess that's the key to what you teach.

Marshall: Everything I do is very simple. There is a common misconception, most of my clients are CEOs or could be CEOs for multibillion dollar companies, and if you've read some of my books, you know who my clients are because they put their names in my books. **Well, the common misconception is that these people would not respond well to simple things and they want complex things; that would be wrong. These people are incredibly busy, and they do not have time for complex things. If it's not positive, simple, focused, and fast, they probably won't do it anyway.** So, I find the higher up you go, the more people that respond to things that are positive, simple, focused, and fast as opposed to complex and convoluted.

Aleks: That's fantastic! So, Marshall, where can people find out more about you?

Marshall: **www.marshallgoldsmithlibrary.com**. Again, I'm Buddhist, I give everything away. All my material people can copy, share, duplicate, use in church, use it in charity, use it anyway you want to use.

Aleks: OK, wow, wonderful! Thank you so much for your time. I really appreciate it.

Marshall: It was great to talk to you!

The Positive Appraisal Process

1. **List Positive Events:** List at least three, preferably four to five, praiseworthy things that you or others have seen them do well.

2. **Give Examples:** Make sure you are genuine with your praise, and give specific (and detailed, if possible) examples of when they have performed each praiseworthy task.

3. **Always Use Empowering Language:** Phrase areas of potential improvement positively. Use terms like "what can be further enhanced, improved, tweaked, modified, and so on."

4. **Find Agreement:** Discuss what has been said, and look for which of your suggestions the other person resonates with most and is most likely to implement.

Advanced Additional Element for Coaches: Have the client rank the order of personal relevance and importance of suggestions given and scale (between 1-10, where 1 = minimal confidence and 10 = maximum confidence) the likelihood of implementation of higher-ranked suggestions. Higher-ranked suggestions with the greatest implementation confidence scores are the ones to focus on.

5. **Future Focused Integration:** Reiterate what they are doing well, praise them again, and have them imagine and feel the benefits of even more improvement by practicing and incorporating the new skills they have chosen to begin developing.

Advanced Additional Element for Coaches: This is where a range of meditative/hypnotic and positive outcome visualization coaching techniques can be used.

After completing the feedback process outlined, the final step is to coach the client in building the new skills required. It is also important that, when offering feedback, the giver of feedback is also in the right emotional and mental frame of mind.

Fantasy Gift – 360-Degree Magic Mirror

You spin me right 'round baby, right 'round, 360 degrees baby, right 'round, 'round, 'round … – because today you've got the incredible opportunity to take home with you our all-new 360-degree MAGIC MIRROR.

In the past, getting feedback was a real struggle. You'd have to find someone who knew what they were doing, then actually shut up, put your ego aside, and listen to them, and then finally, through an ever-so-tedious process of trial and error, implement given suggestions until they became workable.

NOT ANYMORE …

Introducing the "360-degree magic mirror." All you need to do is look into it and it will take care of everything else – AUTOMATICALLY. No more faults, fears of failure, poor performances – all of those PESKY and Pest-Like imperfections will be instantly eradicated.

Here's how it works – simply look into the mirror and our patented SHALLOW-FOCUSED SUGAR-COATING REFLECTIVE-SURFACE TECHNOLOGY will project your ultimate visible self. Then turn the mirror outward, and anyone who comes in contact with your reflected image will be absolutely startled by the image of the incredible person they see before them.

And the best part is, this mirror is compact, so you can take it anywhere. Take it to business meetings, family functions, on dates, in the shower, doctor appointments; even to church … not even the supposedly all-knowing gaze of God can penetrate our patented technology.

So why try and change the hard way? Forget those old ways of listening, learning, and diligently applying with humility. Fast-track your way to perceptual perfection today. Finding fulfillment has never been easier.

And every fan of this book will be going home with their own magic mirror. Just look under your chair, it's right there … congratulations.

Mirror, mirror on the wall, who is the most fabulous of them all?

You are, my new friend, YOU ARE!

The 360 Degree Magic Mirror – what you see is so much more than what you thought you'd get!

Discover your Passions, Build an Authentic Life, and Leave a Legacy

Inspired by the "Sensational Speaker" Tony Alessandra.

Only an authentic life will allow you to leave a legacy worth remembering. By discovering your passions, you can create a life of success and happiness.

I discussed the importance of living an authentic life in a recent interview Dr. Tony Alessandra (pictured left), a business professor, author 27 books and a Hall of Fame keynote speaker. He stated that it was only when he chose to when speaking, that his speaking career and business really took off.

Discovering our real passions in life and expressing our message authentically will allow us to most easily move toward leaving an empowering legacy. However, finding your passions in life is not always easy. It is not an area of life that is taught about at school or in the workplace, and yet it is crucial for true success and happiness.

One could argue that success without passion is a hollow victory. What is the point of being great at something if you don't care about it? That's a big question that a lot of people face in many areas of life. In order to address this fear, after the interview will be a quick three-step process that you can go through to find your passions and add more activities in your life that will cater to your natural loves so you can live more authentically.

In my interview with Tony, you're going to discover ...

- The power of authenticity in business and life
- **A simple technique to help you create an inspiring and lasting legacy**
- Why he rejects many classic "rules" of public speaking
- **The smart way to go find and excel in your natural passions**
- How the one simple change he made in himself transformed his entire speaking career.

Aleks: Hello, and welcome. I'm Aleks George Srbinoski, founder of **FulfillingHappiness.com,** and today my guest is Dr. Tony Alessandra, who has a street-wise, college-smart perspective on business, having been raised in the housing projects of NYC to eventually realizing success as a graduate professor of marketing, entrepreneur, business author, and Hall of Fame keynote speaker. Dr. Alessandra is a prolific author with 27 books translated into over 50 foreign language editions, including the newly revised, best-selling *The NEW Art of Managing People.*

He is featured in over 50 audio and video programs and films and is the originator of the internationally recognized behavioral assessment tool - The Platinum Rule®.

Recognized by *Meetings & Conventions Magazine* as "one of America's most electrifying speakers," Dr. Alessandra was inducted into the Speakers Hall of Fame in 1985. In 2009 and 2010, he was inducted as one of the "Legends of the Speaking Profession," and in 2010 and 2011 he was selected as one of the Top 5 Marketing Speakers by Speaking.com. Tony's polished style, powerful message, and proven ability as a consummate business strategist consistently earn rave reviews and loyal clients. Welcome, Tony.

Tony: Well, thank you, Aleks. I appreciate it.

Aleks: I'm really excited to have you with me today, so let's begin. I'd like to know what was the thought process behind the best life-changing decision you have ever made?

Tony: Well, Aleks, I thought about this question, and I made lot of life-changing decisions that turned out pretty good and some that didn't. But I think one of the best decisions I made was back in 1973, when I decided to go to Georgia State University in Atlanta and get my PhD. *At that time,* I had a master's degree and an MBA, and I was teaching at California State Fullerton, and I decided I really liked university teaching and wanted to continue being a university professor, but the credential that you need to be a university prof is a PhD, so I decided to go back to school.

But going back to get a PhD, I really had to apply to several universities and decide which one was the best, so I applied to several. I wanted to go to a university in an urban environment, maybe because I was born and raised in New York City and I'm an urban person. The university that I actually chose was Georgia State University and the main reason was, I found out that one of their professors in the School of Business and Department of Marketing was Dr. David Schwartz, and it just so happened that one of the life-changing books that I had read when I was younger was called *The Magic of Thinking Big*, and Dr. David Schwartz was the author.

So before I decided to accept going to Georgia State, I called up Dr. David Schwartz on the phone, and I asked him if he would be my dissertation chairperson, and he agreed, and that prompted me to go to Georgia State.

Another big thing of going there was being in an urban university; that led to a lot of sales and marketing and consulting and training. Schwartz was a motivational speaker, and I think that really was what imprinted on me the possibility of being a professional speaker myself. And being there at this urban university had allowed me to start a part-time sales and training company in Atlanta while I was getting a doctorate. And, finally, I knew that having a PhD would become a major credential for me and a differentiator for me in the marketplace. So that was one of the key decisions, it was deciding to go back after I got my MBA and after having three years of university teaching under my belt just with a Master's Degree, to get my PhD.

Now I really think that the second major life changing decision was just two-and-a-half years later after I got my doctorate in 1976 and was deciding to leave university teaching and become a full-time speaker. At that time I was teaching at the University of San Diego. I was teaching professional salesmanship and marketing strategy on the graduate level, but one of the reasons that I have decided to leave university teaching, and I loved it, I really did but I could not stand the petty politics that went on in the university setting with all of these prima donna PhD's complaining about things.

Another part of my thought process was my salary [laughs]. You know, this was back in 1978. I was a PhD, I at the time had eight years of full-time university teaching under my belt, and I was only making $22,000 a year, when in fact part-time consulting and training and speaking was earning me twice that amount. **And I decided I wanted a bit more individual freedom, the ability to work for myself rather than have to work for somebody else like that, and report to the people at the university.**

You know that old saying, "those that can't, teach, and those that can't teach, teach others how to teach?" Well, I wanted to prove to myself and to other people that I could actually excel at what I taught, which was sales and marketing. And I wanted to focus on adult professional education where I could actually see more of an immediate impact of what I was doing. So that was the second big life-changing decision, and I know we only have a couple more minutes, and I wanted to give you the final one.

There's a story that really brought me to where I am today, and that was back in 1982. Now this was, I left university teaching in December '78, went into full-time professional speaking in January '79. And in the summer of 1982, I decided to get some coaching from Bill Gove, who was one of the premier keynote speakers of our time back then. At the time I was brought up well as a speaker, but not great, and I wanted to take my speaking to another level. I wanted to focus on keynote speaking rather than sales training, and so I was looking for another way to define myself in addition to having that PhD.

And during this weekend coaching, Bill Gove said, "Tony, I see your issue. I see your problem. **You were coming across as a professor. That might work at a university but it doesn't work as a keynote speaker."**

He said, **"Tony you are a New York City Italian. You have that mischievous look in your eye. You're always playing practical jokes on people. You are a lot of fun to be around, you're a storyteller. But none of that is coming out in your speeches, and you need to let that come out." So he prompted me, he pushed me.** He prodded me to go out and be more of that New York Italian, and I have to tell you something, Aleks ...

When I changed that style to what Bill Gove told me to do, my speaking career skyrocketed.

So those were three key decisions, life-changing decisions, and some of the thought processes behind it that brought me to where I am today.

Aleks: That's fantastic! Can I ask about that final one? I think you're speaking about authenticity, and how important is authenticity in the world of speaking?

Tony: It's crucial. You know I was friends with people who have gone through the Toastmasters approach, and that person tells you very specific ways to do things and specific ways not to do things.

And the way I spoke, based on my upbringing, my background, my authentic me, I did things that if I had gone through Toastmasters, they would have checked off and said wrong, wrong, wrong. You know, little things like putting my hands in my pocket, just things that they say professional speakers should not do. But it was authentic to who I was, and it helped me connect with the audiences.

And I tell people that they have to make sure that their speaking style, and of course this isn't just for speakers or presenters, it has to be consistent with who they are. Yes, they are a professor, and if that's who they naturally are then that's how they should speak, but I wasn't. I was trying to be something that I thought I should be, when in fact Bill Gove worked me back to being authentic to who I was and how I was brought up.

Aleks: Okay, I think that is really interesting because, yes, you are a professor. You have those qualifications, you have been to university etcetera, but at the same time people need to relate to you and your background and your story, which in some ways is what differentiates you from other people.

Tony: Absolutely, absolutely. You know I grew up in a lower middle class family in the projects of New York City. My father was a New York City cab driver, and that's who I was. My entire family, parents, grandparents, everybody was Italian. I was brought up in an Italian neighborhood. And I just had to let more of that come out, and in a sense I was downplaying it, thinking that I had to come across more professional and professorial. And it was working against me rather than for me.

Aleks: Great! One quick thing before I let you go. What would you advise to someone else in that similar position, where they are struggling to find their feet because perhaps they are trying to be something or do something that is not quite right for them? What advice would you give to them?

Tony: Well, one of the things I tell people to do is to actually write their obituary and in terms of how they would like people to remember them and then to look at that and decide "am I doing now what I would like to be remembered for?" And to start on a process to become what you want your legacy to be. And to get some feedback from other people, find out what you are good at, find out what you are happy doing. And I'm not saying to quit what you're doing now and try to do something brand new overnight. But **if you really want to do something else, whether it's writing, whether it's singing, whether it's speaking, whether it's teaching, it doesn't matter what it is. If you're not doing that now and that is your passion, start on a program today so that within the next three to five years, you can slowly work your way up to being what you truly are meant to be.**

Aleks: That's perfect; that sounds great. So where can people find out more about you, Tony?

Tony: Well a couple of places, Aleks. One would be my personal website which is **www.alessandra.com**. A second site is my more business site which is **platinumrule.com**.

And finally, my assessment business which you can find at **http://assessmentbusinesscenter.com**. So any of those places, you can find out a little bit more about who I am and what I do. And you can find my email address and send me an email.

Aleks: That's fantastic! Thank you so much for your time today.

Tony: My pleasure. Thanks, Aleks.

Pursuing Passions Exercise

Use this simple three step process to uncover your passions and find ways to enjoy more of them in your daily life.

1. Write down everything that you are passionate about. Also write what you could be passionate about (activities you would like to try but are not sure about) and everything that you used to be passionate about when you were younger.

Example – Art, history, music, dancing, interior design, cooking.

2. Write down what qualities need to be within you in order to excel in each area.

Example – Dancing requires rhythm and the ability to follow procedures and rules but still find emotional flair within it, patience, love of movement, etc.

   Interior design in this example probably requires almost all of the same qualities. Of course, some will vary. Then consider and list the qualities required for the others as well, like art, music, cooking, and so on. Clear patterns of qualities will emerge.

3. The final step is to then either schedule more time to do one of the activities that you love or look into finding a new activity that requires similar skills to begin indulging in.

If at any point you are struggling to rank which of your passions are most important to begin with, here are:

Five key questions to ask yourself to know if you are likely to pursue a passion.

Would I do this activity happily for free and even pay to regularly do it and/or get training in it?

Would I want to do this activity even if none of my friends or family were interested in it?

Can I envision myself having moments of great pleasure and/or satisfaction when doing this activity?

Do I feel confident that with the right training and/or effort, I can excel in this activity?

Would I be proud to be known for participating in and possibly excelling at this activity?

Fantasy Gift – Authenuine

Authentic, genuine, honorable! Are all these qualities inside of you waiting to get out?

Not anymore, because you're about to discover the ultimate elixir, something so powerful that just one drink and you will never ever be your guarded self again.

You know that deep down inside you, there is a light, and this light radiates, desperate to burst through you.

But your fears have stifled it. You're just not sure if others will accept this light that comes through you, this light that allows you to express yourself, fully, openly, shamelessly, and passionately.

Well, you don't have to worry anymore.

Introducing our new "True Self Serum — Authenuine." Made from tea tree oil, aloe vera, goji berries, poppy seeds, fungus, and rare desert cacti – not only will this life-enriching liquid fight the 1,700 signs of aging, it will allow you to finally be your true self.

Just one swig, and as soon as our serum enters your bloodstream, you will instantly feel your true self COME ALIVE! You will start to glow, evident by the rosiness of your cheeks, your new inability to notice pain, and the sway of your carefree walk.

To complete the Authenuine experience, add a twist of lemon and a dash of salt to every shot and, to finalize the process, make sure you devour the truth glow worm at the bottom of your bottle.

And please always remember to Drink Responsibly.

And every fan of this book will be going home with their very own case of Authenuine. Just look under your chair; it's right there … congratulations.

Cheers to your true self – out of the bottle and into the real world.

Esteemed Motivation and Business-Building "Success Coach" Outlines a Radical New Formula for Time Management

Introducing the "Motivational Master" himself, Steve Chandler.

Building a successful business in this fast-paced world requires a very different concept of time and possibility. A strictly linear path of time management is likely to leave you left behind. Steve Chandler (pictured left) understands how crucial it is to maximize time through "non-linear" prioritization methods.

Much of the method relates to understanding how to make immediate and valuable connections with clients and prospects in order to drive your business forward. Often, especially in the start-up phase, nothing is a greater use of your time than purposeful client or prospect contact.

In order to prepare to do any task efficiently, it is crucial that you are in the right environment and state of mind. If you are not, you are likely to create an unprofessional impression and, as to be discussed later, first impressions based on "snap judgments" are highly predictive of how future interactions and relationships will turn out.

To assist you, I have outlined a simple five-step priming process to condition you to become more time efficient. It will be revealed after the interview.

In my interview with Steve, you're going to discover ...

- How he turned the principles of psychological warfare into a coaching career
- **New secrets to "non-linear" time management**
- The best way to build a business and immediately connect to prospects
- **How to avoid common pitfalls when starting or building a new business**
- What he did to transform a client's business practices and success in just one session.

Aleks: Hello, and welcome. I'm Aleks George Srbinoski, founder of **FulfillingHappiness.com,** and today my guest is Steve Chandler who is the bestselling author of *100 Ways to Motivate Yourself* and 30 other books that have been translated into over 25 languages.

Known as America's notoriously unorthodox personal growth guru, his personal success coaching, public speaking and business consulting have been used by CEOs, top professionals, major universities, and over 30 Fortune 500 companies.

He has twice won the national Audio of the Year award and King Features Syndicate. A popular guest on TV and radio talk shows, Steve Chandler has recently been called "the most powerful public speaker in America today."

Steve is also a master coach that has helped train hundreds of coaches to transform many lives and businesses. Time now to meet him. Welcome, Steve.

Steve: Thank you very much, thanks for having me.

Aleks: You're more than welcome. Thank you so much for joining me today. So let's get straight into it. I'd like to ask you what was the thought process behind the best life-changing decision you have ever made?

Steve: Well, it really occurred for me many years ago when I was in the military, and I was in a unit called psychological warfare. I had no idea what psychological warfare was, or what they did. I went through some testing when I was in the military. We did some job testing to find what our aptitudes were and what division we would be placed into. And when I got the card back after my testing, there was a word on it that said "psycho," and I thought, "Oh my God, they found me out. I don't know where they're gonna put me now."

And what that really was short for was "psychological warfare," and I went to into that. And when I was in the psychological warfare they did very extensive teaching on how **communication can alter belief systems and how a person's belief systems are fluid; they are not really very firmly tethered down. They are very fluid, and belief systems can be altered quite rapidly through the right kind of communication.** And this is really what psychological warfare is all about.

When I found that out, when I really saw how that worked, I began to see the application of this not in a wartime situation and not in a military situation, but really in lives with individuals. **Individuals who have belief systems that were based on low self-esteem, or a sense of powerlessness, or helplessness, or incompetence, or "I'm not as good as my brother or not as good as other people." These beliefs could actually be deleted and replaced and we could take a creative role in that ourselves.**

And when I got out of the military, got out into life and corrected a few life problems I had – life problems that were debilitating – I began to write books and give talks about it, so that's really where it all began. That's the number one thought process that I went through. It changed how I interacted with the world.

Prior to that time, **I was really a major victim, I was really discouraged, my whole personality was based on skepticism and negative thinking, and so my life turned around a hundred percent, and I thought that if I could do it with myself, I was just**

about the worst case I had ever seen of somebody not really being very creative or being very upbeat. If I could do it with myself, I then knew that I could do it with anybody I worked with, and that turned out to be true.

Aleks: Okay, fantastic. Was it difficult for you to take what you had learned in the military and apply it into a different context?

Steve: No, it wasn't, because I just began experimenting. I began working with people, sitting down with them, listening to them, and applying different experiments with them and talking to them. And I was coaching them before I even knew what coaching was, and then I begin to do some training sessions and I had worked with sales people and leaders, and people who needed to get results, in order to get paid.

So there is always a kind of test for my work that people would pay me for and only if it works. And that was good for me when I started because a lot of people get into the field of self-help and they do all these crazy things, and you never know if it works. You might feel better for a week, but you don't really have any idea if it has really changed your life. And **I always had that standard told to me at the beginning of my work that it really had to change things or I would not be re-hired. And so that was really good for me.**

Aleks: Yeah, I think that's a really important point, which is it has to work, otherwise you are not really doing a great service for yourself, or for the person you are working for.

Steve: Absolutely right. It's absolutely correct, and that's one of the good things about the field that we are in, people who do transformational work and coaching. People who are not effective really at it, they don't get re-hired. They don't get researched. They can get into the work, but then after a while it kind of dries up and goes away for them. So the universe has a sort of sorting out process for people who do this work, and the people whose work really connects really makes the difference, they tend to thrive.

Aleks: So what are the common things that you mostly see, and how do you help people through that?

Steve: Well, the biggest thing I see now is the problem people have with time. And people are using a really outmoded totally traditional but inappropriate time management mindset and belief system. They use all kinds of old fashioned linear time management systems and thought processes.

So **my work with people today is to change that so they can use a totally non-linear time management system, and when they can do that it deals with all the information challenges we have. Because everybody now has more information at their fingertips than anybody ever had, and it's flowing in constantly when people are communicating with us all day long. And that's the biggest challenge we have, but it's also the biggest opportunity we have.**

Aleks: That sounds really fascinating. Could you give me a brief synopsis or example of how your time management ideas not just differ from the norm, but how to apply them in a very quick way?

Steve: Yeah, the way it gets applied in a quick way is, for example, I will work with someone who sits down and tries to plan out a new business or a new coaching career, and this person will start to place all sorts of linear segments in place in the old-fashioned way of thinking. So they will say, "I need a website, I need business cards, I need a brochure, I need a bio, I need a resume, I need certification from a coaching school," and they will actually place all these linear projects between them and success.

So if I take in the nonlinear approach in and **I say to the person, imagine that you have done all these 23 things that you think you need to do, what's the final result hereafter? And the person would say, "My final result is to have a client." Then I'd say, "Great! So let's just call a prospect and turn him into a client." And so what I will do is have my coaching client call someone up on the speaker phone. We will talk to that person for 30 minutes, and now he has a client.**

And I have demonstrated to him that what he thought would take 23 segmented linear steps to get from "A" all the way down to "Z" he can go instead of moving horizontally across the plain, he can rise up vertically and get it done right now. And there are about 50 examples of that every day that we face, where we're using the old-fashioned linear thought process when we could connect with someone immediately and have the result right now that we are looking for.

Aleks: I think you said something very important, connect with someone immediately. Is that the secret?

Steve: That is it. That's really behind everything, that's the secret. And I have written a brand new book about it called *Time Warrior* and I put the word warrior in there because it takes a kind of violence. **You have to be willing to say "no" to all the people who were trying to get your attention and time, and you have to be willing to carve out devoted, quiet, solitude, with full focus on whatever you are focused on so you can achieve things.** Otherwise we're just totally distracted all day long and people think they are being compassionate and loving because they are available to everyone in their lives. But the real problem is they are getting interrupted every few minutes, and they can't hold focus on any one thing long enough to do a great job.

Aleks: Yeah I totally agree with you there. I think that's what has happened with modern technology. Everything is so easily infiltrating into your world, and you have to set aside specific things and get very focused. I think that's what you're saying.

Steve: Exactly right, that's precisely it.

Aleks: Oh, that's fantastic. Well, it's been an absolute pleasure speaking to you. So where can people find out more about you?

Steve: Well, they can go to **stevechandler.com** and that will have my blog and all my latest items that are there and a lot of free materials people can get, so it's very easy.

Aleks: Fantastic! Thank you so much for joining me.

Steve: You're welcome.

The Mental Preparation for Time Efficiency Process

1. Physical Environment Preparation – Clear the Area – Remove all non-essential materials and get them as far away from you as possible. Put them in another room or somewhere where you cannot see them in the room. You can put them in their proper place only if it will not take any extra time. This is not the time for organizing.

Also close down and/or remove all non-essential programs and distractions, and arrange all essential items in preferred position.

2. Clear the Mind – Sit or stand straight with your shoulders back and head up. You can either close your eyes or have them open, but look slightly up and take three deep breaths. With each breath, clear your mind by focusing all your attention on your breath.

This will ground you into the present moment.

3. Praise and Prepare Yourself – Continue sitting straight and breathing deeply. State a positive identity and/or task-based statement. For example, I am a great (smart, skilled, talented, etc.) person about to do an outstanding (wonderful, professional, beautiful, etc.) job for the next 30-60 minutes on X (name task). Say it out loud, write it down in big letters, and place it where it can be easily seen.

4. Clearly Envision the Outcome. Imagine, with as much precision as possible, what you would like to have completed/created 30-60 minutes from now. To increase chances of success, rate the goal on a completion confidence scale between 1-10, where 1 would be very little confidence and 10 would extreme confidence. You should be at least a 7 in confidence. If less than this, reduce aspects of the goal until you are at a 7 or higher. Write down the goal next to your positive statement and your confidence score.

5. Priming the Mind and Emotions – Continuing to sit straight and breathe deeply, close your eyes again if you wish, and create a mental mini-movie of you completing the task. See, hear and feel yourself moving forward through each aspect of the task until it is completed where you feel a sense of accomplishment, pride, strength, or whatever emotion(s) are right for you. Then imagine taking that emotion with you and keeping it as you reverse back through the completed steps until you come back to now. Do that up to two more times, moving forward until task completion and back toward now. *Each time you do this, amplify the internal perceptions and strengthen the positive emotions.* When you have returned to the present moment for the final time, take another deep breath, open your eyes if they are not open already, and begin.

(This entire process should take no more than two minutes if you are writing it down, which is highly recommended. Less than one minute if not).

Fantasy Gift – The Swiss Start Watch

Time is a run-away freight train. It just keeps going and going and going and, whether you like it or not, you're on this ride. But where are you on the train? Are you a passenger or a driver? The train cannot be stopped, but it can be steered.

If only you could find the motivation to get into the driver's compartment. Well, now you can. Pulverize procrastination, maximize momentum, and magnify your motivation all at the exact same time with the new "Swiss Start Watch."

Combining precision Swiss engineering with timeless Texan electro-current technology, the Swiss Start Watch will jolt you into action. As soon as you press the button, a dual electro-current fires off and will not stop until the task you have set out to do … is done!

The first current flows straight into the motivational centers of your brain, making you immediately focused and ready, while the second current seamlessly flows straight to your buttocks, forcing an instant leap into action.

In order to maintain momentum, the self-regulating current naturally adjusts in intensity to keep you active, vibrant, and on track. Finally, get the one motivational tool guaranteed to work every single time. As an additional bonus, you will receive a self-charging lifetime battery, which means you can just set it and forget it because …

Once you start it up, it will never stop … and neither will you.

And every fan of this book will be going home with their very own Swiss Start Watch. Just look under your chair. It's right there … congratulations.

The Swiss Start Watch. A motivational miracle.

Find the Skills required for Monetizing and Breaking into Any New Field by Becoming an Expert and Publishing your Work

Inspired by the "Fearless Freelancer" Eve Adamson.

If you have ever considered developing your skills in a new area, now would be the perfect time. It has never been easier to learn a new skill and embark on a new career. Of course, that does not mean you will be any good or will reach a wide audience, only that it is easier to accomplish. However, if you are truly motivated to become an expert in your chosen field, then great opportunity awaits.

According to freelance author of over 65 books Eve Adamson (pictured above), part of knowing how to break into a new field is being very aware of your current skills and future requirements for success. Success demands you to truly examine yourself and create the right kind of internal pressure in order to begin forging a new career path.

Part of the requirement is that you find and work to truly understand your field of endeavor. To assist you with such a process, after the interview you will receive a four-step solution.

In my interview with Eve, you're going to discover ...

- The three key considerations required to become successful in a new field
- **What she did to generate the internal pressure needed to go after her dreams**
- The one thing you must be confident about before becoming an entrepreneur
- **The specific process behind her most transformative life decision**
- How to avoid the most common pitfalls of the new entrepreneur.

Aleks: Hello, and welcome. I'm Aleks George Srbinoski, founder of **FulfillingHappiness.com** and today my guest is Eve Adamson, who is a 5 time *New York Times* best-selling author and freelance writer who has written or co-authored over 65 books. She is an in demand *celebrity ghostwriter* and has written hundreds of magazine articles on subjects as varied as yoga, stress management, Zen, healthy diets, cooking, holistic health, chakra exploration, dream interpretation, animal companion care, and green living.

Celebrities and experts hire her to help them write their books, and Eve has the unique gift of hearing a client, knowing who that person is, and translating what they say into the book of their dreams. A serious student of yoga and meditation, Eve believes that experiencing the journey of another is a way to experience the self. So first of all, welcome Eve.

Eve: Thank you very much.

Aleks: Thank you. Sounds like quite a bio you have; it sounds like you have you have quite a lot of experience writing your own books and others. Great to have you on board.

Eve: Thank you, I have a lot of experience *now*, after many years, and it wasn't always that way, but yeah.

Aleks: Fantastic, so let's get straight to it. Eve, what was the thought process behind the best life-changing decision you have ever made?

Eve: Well, the decision, choosing the decision to discuss with you, was easy and that decision was back at the beginning of my career: Could I do it? Could I quit a sensible job and regular employment with pay checks and benefits, insurance, all those things, and be a freelance writer? Could I do that? Could I actually step out of the cubicle and the working world and work for myself and actually make that work? At the time that was a terrifying process, and I get a lot of people who come up and ask me about this very question because they want to do it but they're afraid.

It was a big decision, and so I thought I'd tell you how I made that decision. I had always wanted to be a writer, and when I was a child I would write stories all the time, read books, and even write melodramatic novellas to exercise my teenage angst. And then I went on to college and was an English major, and then I went on to graduate school and got a Masters in Fine Arts and Creative Writing.

But once I was out in the world I was unsure how to proceed, and the only thing that I really knew how to do at that time that was marketable was type very quickly. So, I was working as a word processor in an office for doctors and transcribing clinic notes in a fast way and really not writing at all. And like many people who get out of writing programs, I just wasn't sure what to do. I knew I needed to pay the bills and make a living.

But then I had a baby and that was the first step toward changing everything because it changed my mindset. **Suddenly, putting a child into day care for 10 hours a day while I worked in a cubical at a job that I didn't love was no longer a viable option. It was one thing to compromise my own dreams for a pay check but suddenly the landscape had changed. So that was my first clue that maybe there was another option for me, so I started to look into other options.**

I always heard about freelance writing, and it always seemed like something impossible. I didn't know anyone who did it. I couldn't imagine how it was done. But once I had that baby in my arms I thought, "Well, what if I could do that? What if I could work from home?" I had an MFA in poetry writing, which is much different than making a living at writing. Obviously, poetry is not the most lucrative type of writing out there.

Aleks: Really? I didn't know that ... (laughs)

Eve: (laughs) But I thought, you know, I wrote a lot of papers in English, I wrote essays, I know how to write. I'm trained in writing, maybe I could try this. So, I was terrified because there was no regular pay check. **There was no guarantee. While I was married at the time and there was a second income, which made it a little easier, I was still afraid because I had always been the primary wage earner, and yet there was that baby and I thought you know what, I think I'm going to try this.**

Now, this is kind of the first part, it wasn't the really big part of the decision. I started to do it and I met with some modest success after a year or two, and just as I was kind of starting to get some regular assignments and do it, I got divorced. Suddenly the game changed again.

There was no second income. I had had a second baby, and it was me and two small children. Then I felt myself at the edge of this metaphorical cliff. I thought, I could step back into safety, I could get a regular job with insurance and all of those things, or I could jump and hope that I could quickly learn to fly on the way down.

It was terrifying, but my thought process was this ... first of all, **number one, I had the training.** I knew how to write. I knew that I was schooled in it. I knew that I was good in it. I had confidence in my ability to write well.

Number two, I had the motivation. I still wanted to be home with these children and raise them myself, and I had never had a lot of success having a boss over me telling me what to do. I've always been a little more comfortable telling myself what to do.

I had the training and motivation, but my big problem was did I have the guts. Did I have the guts to do it? Now a lot of people ask, "Did you have a backup plan? Did you have a job lined up on the side just in case for that extra money? Did you have a job waiting for you just in case it didn't work out?"

That was my decision, this was the big question: what if I purposely did not have a backup plan? **If I did not have a backup plan, I would have to make this work. I would have to make my dream work. I would have no choice, and it took me a couple weeks of deliberation but I finally decided, you know what? I'm going to do it. I'm going to jump. I have the skills. All I have to do is jump and without a backup plan, I will have to make it work. I think because I put that pressure on myself, it generated enough energy internally within me to make it work.**

Aleks: Okay, so it's kind of like I'm just going to burn the bridges so I have no other choice than to make this work.

Eve: It was a dream that I thought was still impossible. **There was so much competition out there, and once you get to that point where you know you are good at something and you have the guts, you realize there isn't that much competition. Most people don't get to that level, most people don't jump so once you've jumped, the field is fairly clear out there and you've got a lot of room to fly** and so it happened for me and like I said, I knew no one else who had done this. I figured it all out by myself, but it was knowing I had that training behind me and then having that courage. I'm going to jump without a backup plan that made that decision possible, and so I did it and I've never looked back.

There were those moments where I didn't know where the next check would come from, and I thought did I make a terrible mistake, but I never gave into that fear, and I always pushed through the fear and it always works itself out. It's been completely worth that risk because I refuse to give in and not have that backup plan and I made a successful and somewhat rare career for myself, I think, because I made that decision.

Aleks: Wonderful. So there's a couple things I just want to mention. First thing is you said you raised your standards after having a child. You felt that even if you don't deserve more or you felt that at the time, you felt *they* deserved more, would that be true?

Eve: Well, I thought they deserved me.

Aleks: Yes.

Eve: They deserved to have me with them. They deserve to have their mother at home with them and so yes, I wanted them to have the life I knew was right for them and so that was huge … The passion generated from that feeling was a huge motivation and even helping me to see that this decision existed in the first place.

Aleks: Wow. Finally, what advice would you give to someone else who finds themself in a similar position you were in?

Eve: Well, I have a lot of people come and ask me that and say they are in this situation. One of the reasons I wanted to **emphasize that I have the training first, was because a lot of people want to freelance or set their own business because they have this idea, this romanticized idea of it. You have to have the training part first behind you** if you want … for instance, in my case if you want to be a writer, you have to know how to write.

It's a skill you have to learn, and it takes a lot of practice. So, you have to have that part behind you but if you know that you have that … if you know that you are good at the thing you want to do then it really takes the courage. **You have to be willing to step out on that ledge and go for it because if you do have that backup plan, it's so easy when things get tough to fall back and say, "Oh, this is too stressful, I'm just going to go back to this other job," but if that's not there, that's what forces you to push through and make it work for yourself.**

Otherwise, so many people, I can't tell you how many hundreds of people I know who have given up and gone back to the safety of their backup plan because it was too scary. If you don't have that lack of a security safety net behind you, you have to keep going forward, and that's how you become successful beyond what is normal. That's how you reach that dream that most people never reach.

Aleks: Wow, that's fantastic. Thank you so much, Eve. Where can people find out more about you?

Eve: You can go to my website. It's **www.eveadamson.com**. I'm often updating it. It has a lot of the books I've published and written for other people and some of the articles. I keep adding more to it as I keep doing more things.

Aleks: Wonderful, thank you so much.

Eve: Thank you.

Finding the Right Training and Building a
Business Model around Your Passions Process

1. Brainstorm and Select – Write down a list of your personal and professional interests. Then choose the one thing you would like to learn more about and/or learn how to turn into a business.

2. Research – Go to your preferred internet search engine and type in key phrases related to your area. Examples are:

How to make money doing X (Choose your main passion - e.g., selling recipes, writing fiction, interior design, dance teaching, graphic design, fitness/sport instructing, self-development, programming, marketing, advertising, business development, social media, sowing, antiquing, art, etc)

How to become a successful X

How to make money by being an expert on X

Who are the best (leaders) at X

Training courses in X

3. Sifting and Culling – Gather the top 10-20 applicable search results for each key phrase. Before purchasing anything, examine all the free information across all the categories. Be aware that much of it may be of poor quality, which is why you need to look at all of it. Then look at the biographies and successes about the person/company who has created the information. Cull mercilessly and create a short list of potential programs.

4.   **Decide on the Best Fit** – Choose only one program and commit to completing it fully before considering anything else. Look for the program/person that best compliments your values, ideas, beliefs, and budget. Be realistic with your budget; don't just go for the cheapest or the most expensive option. Balance all the factors, especially the credibility of the program.

Additional points:

(a) To be safe, whatever timeframe or cost is associated with success, triple it.

(b) If you really want local, hands-on or one-on-one training, go through the same process, but click on local search options on your internet search or add the name of your town in your key phrase searches.

Fantasy Gift – The Auto-Writer Gloves

So many of us dream of becoming experts with best-selling books to our name, but who wants to write? Being cooped up in a room all by yourself with nothing but you and the blank page. Could you imagine anything more depressing? You know you're brilliant, you know there is so much untapped potential burning inside of your unconscious mind begging to come out. Well, now it can!

The "Auto-Writer Gloves" are the perfect fit for your creative process. Designed by members of the once-secret, now-defected "New York Times Science and Narrative Propaganda Division," these gloves are guaranteed to guide you in writing your best seller with no effort. In fact, you don't even need to be awake. Just put a keyboard on your lap as you go to sleep, and let the soothing sounds of computer keys lull you to sleep while your fingers and unconscious mind take care of the rest.

Imagine the smile on your face as you awaken every morning with another high-quality chapter completed and ready to go to the printer. It's time to show the world what you can do. Do not let any lack of writing skill, talent, or knowledge interfere with your dreams. Your subconscious mind will provide the raw material, and the auto-writer will take care of the rest. Order your set of gloves now: blue for self-development, red for business, white for fiction, and a range of others for every type of writing you need. Becoming an internationally renowned expert leader in your field has never been so easy.

And everyone who purchases these will also receive the just released auto-PR phone system, giving you direct phone access to all the producers of all the biggest shows. Get ready to get more publicity than a presidential sex scandal, guaranteed.

The world is at your fingertips.

And every fan of this book will be going home with their very own set of auto-writer gloves. Just look under your chair. They're right there … congratulations.

The auto-writer gloves. Write your story today.

How to Grow Stronger, Smarter, Wiser, and More Successful As You Age, No Matter How Old You Are – and Change Your Future

With the "Classic Books Connoisseur" Tom Butler-Bowdon.

Age is no barrier to success. Unless of course, you believe it is. In a world overflowing with poor role models, sifting through the endless stream of negative news and fear campaigns around age can leave even the strongest-willed person feeling demoralized.

However, there are many incredible examples of success by people of all ages as was expressed by self-help classics research guru Tom Butler-Bowdon (pictured left). Having avidly studied the entire self-development industry for years, he knows that, although success takes a good deal of time to cultivate, it is very much possible – even in later decades of life – if you are committed to the process.

I personally could not agree more and once wrote an article about the very inspirational 82–year-old 2012 Oscar-winning actor Christopher Plummer, whose career success and recognition is peaking while he is in his 80s. In order to help you decide whether currently changing your life direction is a wise idea, I have outlined a four-step process to assist you to "see" into your future. It will be revealed to you after the interview.

In my interview with Tom, you're going to discover ...

- The power of "the 10-year rule"
- **After researching hundreds of books, he gives away his top secret to personal development success**
- Why age is no barrier to success
- **How to overcome the biggest self-development myth**
- Information about building inspiration and maintaining motivation by knowing how to give yourself the right time frames.

Aleks: Hello, and welcome. I'm Aleks George Srbinoski, founder of **FulfillingHappiness.com** and today my guest is Tom Butler-Bowdon, who is a graduate of the London School of Economics and the University of Sydney. Tom was working as a political advisor in Australia when, at 25, he read his first personal development book. Captivated by the genre, his view was that this is an underrated field of writing.

At 30, he left his first career to write the bestselling 50 Self-Help Classics, the first guide to the personal development literature and winner of the Benjamin Franklin Award in 2004.

This book was followed by 50 Success Classics, 50 Spiritual Classics, 50 Psychology Classics, and 50 Prosperity Classics. With commentaries on over 250 books in the self-development field, the series has been published in 21 languages and is sold in over 30 countries. Tom has been described by USA Today as "a true scholar of this type of literature."

He has given talks to a variety of groups and organizations and also leads discussion groups where he lives in Oxford (UK), looking into the major writings and ideas in personal development. He is contracted to write a motivational work for Virgin Books entitled Never Too Late to Be Great, due for publication in January 2012 (now released).

Tom's website, with its wealth of free self-development content, has had over two million visits since its launch in 2001. Welcome, Tom.

Tom: Welcome, Aleks. Great to be here.

Aleks: Thank you. First of all let me say, 50 thank yous for joining me today.

Tom: (laughs) Thanks very much.

Aleks: Okay, let's begin. What was the thought process behind the best life-changing decision you have ever made?

Tom: Well, it really goes back to some of the comments you've made already about my background. I was in government work in Sydney a few years back, and I started reading some of these personal development books and thought, "Wow." They really blew me away.

But I had a very good career ahead of me. You know, with all the perks and pension and everything. And I was set to go and study in London to do a Master's degree. But I started getting really into the personal development field and it suddenly occurred to me, "Hey, this could become a career," and that was a pretty way out thought at that time because I had this solid career ahead of me in government work and political economy.

But I started to think, well … **If I look back on my life in a few years' time, would I regret not going into this area that really fired me up. So, even though it seemed pretty way out at the time, I made a decision to ease myself away from the government career I was in and really go "full ball" into exploring self-development.**

I didn't really know what I wanted to do at that time. All I could think of was, "Hey, there are so many great classic books out there and no one has really written about them." So, to me it just seemed obvious at that time.

And what I tell people now always is, **do what seems obvious to you. Even though you think it's the obvious thing to do because you are unique, most other people would have not thought of it.** So to me, it seemed obvious that there was no guide to the whole self- development, motivational literature out there. And so I set about writing one basically and that became the first book, *50 Self-Help Classics*.

And, it was a few years before it became a proper full-time career for me. **So for anyone listening, you have to factor in a certain amount of lead time. But things do come to fruition.**

And I guess all the success I've had to date in my new career goes back to this original decision which was a bit of a leap of faith, I guess, to leave my existing career and jump into something totally unknown where I had no contacts, skills, background, or anything. But it's paid off.

Aleks: What is it about personal development that has attracted you to it and keeps attracting you to it?

Tom: It is the idea that the world, reality, actually ... **that most people have no real inkling of what they are capable of. They just push along in the same old career path trying to make small incremental changes, you know, a little bit of a raise here, a bit more knowledge here, but the whole idea of personal development is that you can make significant major changes**.

They don't happen all at once, but, **after a 10-year period, for instance, you can look back and think, "God that's incredible progress that I made."** So I guess the real enticement for me is the fact that most people don't really realize what they are capable of. And the personal development field aims to bring that out. And I guess that's what really got me fired up in the first place about it.

Aleks: How did you surprise yourself?

Tom: I surprised myself by working out that, **you don't have to have any great contacts or connections with the field; that the key thing is to give yourself enough time. You know, you have heard about the 10-year rule. I gave myself 10 years to really do something substantial in this area. And I think it's true that people say you should think in terms of decades and not years.**

And you know, even though it seems incremental to me, what I have achieved, when I look back where I was when I first finished that Master's degree and thought, "Oh, I am going into this field." It's amazing progress. So for me, the **whole missing link in the personal development field is the appreciation of time. Everything is about "change your life in seven days," "change your life in a month." When people give themselves a long enough time frame to achieve things then everything becomes possible.**

Aleks: I absolutely agree with you, and I think it's one of the reasons why I am enjoying speaking to you. Because you obviously have a very methodical and measured and realistic (and at the same time ambitious) approach to life, and self-development, and moving forward. So I am wondering, how do you translate that idea which isn't as sexy as "change your life in seven days" to people?

Tom: Well, what I'm putting in this book, *Never Too Late to be Great* is just the sheer **volume of examples of famous, great, remarkable people, who didn't really get into their stride until their late 30s, 40s, 50s, and 60s even. People like Ray Kroc who started McDonald's when he was 52, the guy who started Red Bull, I think he was 43. Even in the internet computer world, like Jimmy Wales starting Wikipedia when he was 35. Craigslist's founder, he was well into his 40s.**

So what excites me and what I think I can convey is the idea of **achieving everything you want by the time you are 22 or even 30, is just such a myth. And, for people to hang on to that, for me, it's just a dead end. But when you look at the hundreds of examples of people who didn't really get into their stride until later on, you realize that is the reality, that is the 99% of people's experience. And people, if you give yourself enough time, a few decades to really do everything you want to do, not only is it possible, it's probable, okay!** Give yourself enough time, and it's probable. We are all living much longer now, so you know there are no real excuses for not doing what you really want to do.

Aleks: I agree with you. What I am wondering then is, how do you ... I mean obviously, you've talked about the importance of the length of time, so how important is the process? You must love the process, knowing that it's not going to happen overnight in most cases?

Tom: Yeah. You do have to live in the present. You do have to enjoy the work that you are doing, day to day. If you hate your work, there's no point to it, even if you can achieve something in it. **You've got to enjoy what you are doing every day.** I mean, I enjoy writing for few hours a day. I enjoy the actual process, even though it's difficult sometimes. I've got a painter friend of mine and I said to him, you just hang out for the final product or ... And he said ... "No, no, I love putting the paint on the canvas." **So, you got to live in day-type compartments of enjoying what you do in the moment. But it's through that enjoyment that you can actually create something great over the long term.**

Aleks: Fantastic. Before I let you go, what is one thing that you would take away? You have done all this research, you studied all these classic books. What is one piece of information that really struck you through all the research and all the readings that you have done?

Tom: It's **not to let yourself and your mind get taken over by the world's prevailing ideas or other people's negative ideas. It's to realize that, through your thoughts you actually create your world,** and that has been said many times in the motivational literature and so on that it's such a cliché.

But when you actually try to live it every day, you find that it's so true.

And that's why people get into things like affirmation and visualization. It's based on the idea that **you can create your own world. You engineer it through your thinking and through your actions, and your thoughts, and your speech every day.** And, it took me a long time to actually put that into practice. Once you do, you realize it has incredible effect.

Aleks: That's wonderful. Where can people find out more about you, Tom?

Tom: You can just Google me: Tom Butler-Bowdon, and I've got a website with books and so on. And, you can just also type in "50 classics" as a search term, you'll find me.

Aleks: Okay, great. And I have your website here, **Butler-Bowdon.com**, is that correct?

Tom: Yeah, that's correct.

Aleks: Thank you so much for your time today.

Tom: Thanks a lot, Aleks. It was a pleasure.

Change Your Future Exercise

This exercise works on the assumption that you feel you need to take a new direction in your life and have some ideas in mind about what you would like to pursue. (If you do not know what you would like to pursue and need help discovering it, see previous exercises).

1. Clear the mind – Sit or stand straight with your shoulders back and head up. You can either close your eyes or have them open, but look slightly up and take three deep breaths. With each breath, clear your mind by focusing all your attention on your breath.

This will ground you into the present moment.

2. Open your mind to worst-case future scenario (based on the change you want to make). Spend up to one minute imagining a movie where you can see, hear, and feel the progression of your life up to 10 years from now, and imagine nothing has gone right. Although you have periods where you feel engaged in what you are doing (because you are passionate about it), you have achieved no external signs of success and may even have gone backwards in terms of finances, relationships, and health.

This is the worst-case scenario and the question is: could you still live with this possibility 10 years from now? Would following your passion still have been worth it?

Contrast this with the, *keep doing what you are doing now worst-case future scenario*. Spend up to one minute imagining a movie where you can see, hear, and feel the progression of your life up to 10 years from now, and imagine things have continued to deteriorate. You rarely feel happy any of the time, and you have achieved little or no additional external signs of success. You may even have gone backwards in terms of finances, relationships, and health.

Could you still live with this possible scenario 10 years from now? Compare it to the first.

3. Open your mind to a mild to moderate success-only scenario where you made this change going into the future. Spend up to one minute imagining a movie where you can see, hear, and feel the progression of your life up to 10 years from now and imagine only mild to moderate success. Although you have periods where you feel engaged in what you are doing (because you are passionate about it), you have not hit the big-time in any way, and you have had many ups and downs and know there are many more to come.

How does it feel to live with this possible scenario 10 years from now?

Contrast this scenario of *achieving mild to moderate success only with the, what you are doing now future scenario*. Spend up to one minute imagining a movie where you can see, hear, and feel the progression of your life up to 10 years from now, and imagine things have continued to move along steadily in the expected way. You rarely feel happy much of the time, but you have continued to satisfactorily progress at work, and you are likely to have progressed in terms of income. You may or may not have progressed in terms of overall finances, relationships, and health.

Could you still live with this possible scenario 10 years from now? Compare it to the one before it.

4. Open your mind to a high to very high success scenario in the future that came from making this change. Spend up to one minute imagining a movie where you can see, hear, and feel the progression of your life up to 10 years from now and imagine high to very high success. You have regular periods where you feel engaged in what you are doing (because you are passionate about it), and although there may have been numerous ups and downs, you have achieved a high to very high level of success and are confident of further growth.

How does this possible scenario feel 10 years from now?

Contrast this scenario of achieving high to very high success with the, what you are doing now future scenario. Spend up to one minute imagining a movie where you can see, hear, and feel the progression of your life up to 10 years from now, and imagine things have continued to move along in a best-case scenario type of way. You rarely feel happy much of the time doing what you do, but you have great signs of external success and have progressed in terms of income, but may or may not have progressed in terms of overall finances, relationships, and health.

Could you still live with this possible scenario 10 years from now? Compare it to the one before it.

You now have a great idea of what your future can hold. You just need to decide on what you want to do.

Fantasy Gifts – Decade into Day Compressor

As we go through life, life, life, we age, age, age, and we may lose faith in our dreams. We learn, but we don't realize just how tough it's going to be.

Well, you can just skim over the toughest bits and have full, immediate, and gratifying success right now, today.

Just like a movie, we have the technology that can elegantly pull you through all the hard, tough, and nasty bits associated with pursuing authentic living in just 3 1/2 minutes by using the power of an intellectual montage accompanied by an inspirational background song of your choosing.

That's right, we can just gloss over years of grinding challenges and setbacks in just 3.5 minutes, and then spend the rest of this 20-minute-only process filling your mind with the information and EXPERIENCE you need for total success.

Using patented matrix-inspired info-experiential download technology (it's just like that famous scene in the movie *The Matrix* where she downloads a program directly into her brain and can fly a helicopter immediately afterward), we, too, can directly download 10 years of learning into your brain in just minutes.

We call it the "Decade into Day Compressor" and, with it, success is guaranteed. Why actually spend 10 years learning your craft when we can give you everything you need for total, unquestionable and undeniable fulfilment through our pain-free system?

Success: it's less than a day away.

And every fan of this book will be going home with their very own Decade Into Day Compressor. Just look under your chair. It's right there … congratulations.

Enjoy putting the fun back into fulfilment.

Have You Taken the Time to Go to the FREE Extra Resources Page?

As much fun as reading this book is, I am sure you have a reason for why you got it. You have this book because you want to live life on your terms, follow your passions and build a business.

That is why if you haven't already, make sure you take the opportunity now to jump onto the free extra resources page.

I want to help you overcome your greatest challenges by giving you:

- **All 11 radio show/seminars on which this book is based**
- Bonus Interviews
- **A High Level Goal Setting Process**
- Cheat Sheets and Templates
- **Fast and focused self-development techniques**
- And More…

Get in while their still hot off the downloadable presses:
FulfillingHappiness.com/dddbonuses

The 80/20 Principle in Action

With the "Bold Business Builder," Richard Koch.

Setting up a new business is a terrifying endeavor. Many of the shadier business types like to tell you it is easy. They propose to have simple shortcuts, outsourced staff, and guaranteed automation with push-button set-and-forget solutions. When you speak to a real entrepreneur with an incredible track record of success, you tend to find the story is a little different.

As the author of *The 80/20 Principle*, Richard Koch (pictured left) understands what is required for real success. . In simple terms, the 80/20 principle suggests 80% of results come from 20% of causes. Therefore, if you can find and harness that top 20%, you are going to excel well beyond the competition. The bad news is it can take real effort to find and harness the top 20%. The good news is you don't have to find it alone.

If we surround ourselves with the best people, such as the top 20% of a particular industry or group, then finding superior solutions becomes much easier. In my interview with Richard Koch, you discover just how he did that. A large part of the process for finding the top 20% of people is trusting your intuition based on first impressions. These are called "snap judgments," and they tend to be quite accurate when properly followed. After the interview, you will find a process to help you learn how to review first impression encounters and better create your own first impressions.

In my interview with Richard, you're going to discover ...

- Key mindset elements required to start a new business
- **How he used university students to build his first extremely profitable business**
- The best way to niche a new business and reduce chances of failure
- **What kind of people to hire and why company culture is more important than staff intelligence**
- The most important characteristics to look for when partnering with others or hiring staff.

Aleks: Hello, and welcome. I'm Aleks George Srbinoski, founder of **FulfillingHappiness.com** and today my guest is Richard Koch, who gave up life as a highly successful consultant at the age of 40 to become an entrepreneur. He has been a co-founder of several new businesses including Belgo (a restaurant chain in London) and LEK Consulting and greatly assisted with the expansion of others like Betfair. He also has turned around nearly-bankrupt companies such as Filofax and Plymouth Gin. He remains an investor in new ventures and has developed a template for changing the odds of success – he only invests in what he calls "network stars," businesses that are the leaders in fast-growth network niches.

For the last 15 years he has also written a book each year – books about ideas that help people improve their happiness and results. His biggest hit remains *The 80/20 Principle*, which has sold more than three quarters of a million copies and has been translated into 34 languages. His latest book is called *The 80/20 Manager*. Time now to meet him. Welcome, Richard!

Richard: Hello, thanks very much. Lovely introduction, thank you, Aleks.

Aleks: You're more than welcome. It's quite impressive, so I'm really glad to have you on board.

Richard: It's a pleasure to be with you and to everyone who is tuning in by whatever means, that's great.

Aleks: Fantastic, so let's get straight down to business. The question I have for you is what was the thought process behind the best life-changing decision you have ever made?

Richard: Well, I think that the best decision I have ever made was to go into business on my own account as a Strategy Consultant. But I have to say that thinking is probably dignifying it a little bit ... I was working for about **eight years before I actually started my own, or co-started my own firm, and during the whole of that time there was just one thought that just kept re-occurring me to me: it would be a lot more fun and a lot more profitable if I was able to be one of the founders of one of these firms.**

I mean, this was the time when strategy consulting was quite new and businesses such as Bain and Company were going at 40% a year. It was just a **very interesting business to be in, but it was even more interesting if you were the boss of it, if you were able to take the company and decide who you would hire and decide which kinds of clients to go for and which products and services you would provide.**

So, I actually, from the time I started strategy consulting was pretty determined to be one of the founders of the companies. I didn't want to do it on my own because I didn't actually enjoy the administrative side of things. I didn't actually want to be running things or deciding who is to get paid what and all that sort of stuff. I wanted to go into business with probably one or two other partners. So, I was always looking out for who might be suitable.

And that opportunity came about in a very oblique way. One Saturday morning in 1983 I was talking on the phone to one of the people who worked for me as a manager at Bain and Company.

I was then a newly promoted Vice President of Bain and Company, and we were talking about this, that, and the other and a piece of work which we were doing.

And at the end of the conversation he said to me, "Have you heard about Jim and Iain?" Jim and Iain were colleagues of ours who were at the same level as me as Vice Presidents of Bain and Company. They were a couple people that I had thought of in the back of my mind as prospective partners for a consultant business, but we'd never discussed it and Bain and Company was very strict in many ways. You wouldn't talk about something like that idly because you know – no one had ever left the company, no one has ever spun off from the company to start another business.

It was not something that the big boss at Bain and Company at the time, Bill Bain at the time, would have encouraged so there was almost a Stalinist tinge to it. Anyway this chap Iain Fisher said to me, "Have you heard about Jim and Iain?" And I said, "No, I haven't!" And it so happens that Iain was in Boston at the time. Well he said, "I can't tell you about it but it's really, really bad." You know, he wouldn't say any more than that and I said, "Well, this is very strange." So, I thought I would contact Jim and Iain, and I rang their homes and all three of us were living in London at the time. So, I rang the homes and the phone was busy engaged.

Basically, they wouldn't answer the phone. Then, I thought, well I'm going to have to go and try to find them so I got on my bicycle – I lived in Bayswater near Hyde Park – and cycled quite a distance out to Richmond, which was where Iain Evans actually lived, and I found them together and then they told me a remarkable story which was that they had gone to Boston to resign from Bain and Company to set up a consulting business.

They thought it was polite to go and tell Bill Bain why it was that they were going to do that. But he then kept them talking and eventually a Federal Marshal walked in the room and slapped an injunction, a lawsuit which said that you couldn't start a business because we will sue the hell out of you if you do that. And they travelled back overnight, arrived back in Iain's house and they were basically feeling extremely depressed and wondering should we go ahead or not go ahead.

So, I said, "Look, this is great. You've got long faces, but I think this is a great idea and we should do it, and if you're interested I would be very happy to be a partner of yours." And I think that's what pulled them out of their depression. They went away for a huddle in a separate room and decided that yes, in principle they would want to do that. It was a few months before we actually in the end set up together, and that was the start of it. It really did change my professional life.

The best thing was actually being able to hire the people you wanted, and I went and hired, I remember, the second year we were going it had been just over a year, I went to Oxford and Cambridge and hired undergraduates, people that were about to graduate and I hired 30 of the best people that I could find who struck me as high energy and extremely intelligent and very nice people.

Aleks: Wow, that's brilliant.

Richard: ... and so, I hired those people and since then many of them have left us; they've become heads of corporations. One of them is the head of Permira, which is a big private equity firm which he has made very successful. **That network of people has really been the best thing in my life in terms of friendships and in terms of business subsequently. But, all of the investments ideas which I got, I got from people who were part of that network.**

It was fabulous. It was a once in a lifetime experience, but I guess my only point would be **you can make a decision but the opportunity may come up sort of when you least expect it and you've got to be looking for it. In the back of your mind, you've got to be thinking** *could this possible be my big break.*

Aleks: Right. There are just a couple things I want to follow up on. One thing is I really like the idea of finding the best people you can find who are ready to be moulded and ready to learn, and you went into Oxford, you said?

Richard: Yes, Oxford and Cambridge.

Aleks: So you went to Oxford and Cambridge and actually just did a big sweep and tried to grab as many talented people as you could that are ready to learn and get out there.

Richard: Yeah, at the time **we had about 13 people in the whole firm so I actually did a little trick on my partners. I said, "I'm going to make 30 offers but of course you understand at most that only half of them will accept because we are in competition with McKinsey, BCG and Bain and other companies and who's heard of us? We're a tiny little company and you know, and are they going to take the risk of joining us." Out of 30 people, 28 accepted and my partners looked at me and said, "We can't employ 28 people!" I said, "Yes, we can. Let's do it." Of course, we found work for them to do.**

The great thing is to actually choose who you work with is fantastic. One of the things that I learned from the **Boston Consulting Group was that they went after purely 'A' people, and there was no professional in the whole Boston Consulting Group who wasn't truly remarkable in terms of intellect. That's what they went after, and I wanted to do it not just for intellect but for other things as well.** But, to actually be able to select people you work with and to get them to come and join you. Particularly, when they're young I think is one of the most wonderful things you can do.

Aleks: Right, so shaping their future basically.

Richard: Right, and shaping the future of the firm by hiring people. **We also had this policy to only hire the best and you know after a time one or two people decided it wasn't for them or we decided that although they were very intelligent, they didn't fit into the culture or the firm or whatever. But, by and large, the people I hired were there several years and became very good friends.**

Aleks: Wonderful. Well, we're almost out of time, so just very quickly, what would you advise for someone else who is at that point where they want to take the big plunge into something important to themselves like a business? What would you advise just before we wrap up?

Richard: I think it's very important to choose the right business, frankly. I mean I think it's great to start a business but, as you know, most businesses fail. **I believe that the way to be successful is to take a variant of an existing successful business. So, something you see as successful, in another geography or something that is quite close to what you do. You've got the be confident that there's going to be a market and that it's going to grow fast, and if you're confident in that then you've got to also tweak whatever it is you do so you do something that no one else does.** I guess, that's it. But, think extremely carefully about the business. There are probably a zillion different businesses that you could decide to enter; you've got to choose the right one.

Aleks: Wonderful, thank you so much for your time Richard!

Richard: It's a pleasure, and nice talking to you, and good luck to everyone out there. Good luck and thanks.

Aleks: And for those who would like to find out more about Richard, they can visit **richardkoch.net** and follow him on Twitter via @RichardKoch8020.

Snap Judgments Review and Creation Process

Key: Ensure you answer every question and sub-question set out in the following process, using a previously important interaction and/or event as the source.

1. Review Emotions – Tune in to how you felt during the event. What were you feeling when with him or her? Did you feel more positive emotions like excited, energetic, comfortable, joyful; or more negative emotions like uncertain, bored, edgy, or disappointed?

2. Review Physicality – How frequent was eye contact? How close did you sit or stand to each other, and how did it feel? Did one of you pull back or edge forward as it progressed? Was body language open or closed, and was there any physical contact? How did the conversation feel and sound? Did it seem respectful, fun, and flowing or was it stilted and awkward?

3. Quality of Contact – What was the quality of the physical contact (handshake or hand on shoulder), if any? Whether you touched each other or not, did it feel right as an idea? Did they look you in the eyes when shaking your hand or away? Did they smile or did it seem more obligatory? Were they simply going through the motions, or did it feel genuine? Did the contact, if made, feel right in regard to firmness?

4.* OPTIONAL: What could you have done differently to have enhanced the interaction? Could you have smiled more, spoken with more authority or less, listened more, engaged in more eye contact, changed your body language, touched more or less, and so on? From all these considerations, choose three in particular and consciously aim to use them in your next important set of interactions.

Fantasy Gift – Best People Magnet

Your life and your business success will be determined by the people around you. But how do you know if the people working for you are the best available? Sometimes it only takes one bad egg to destroy an entire business. Even with a lengthy interview processes, psychometric tests, and your own finely tuned gut instinct, you still never know if you're working and creating friendships with the right people.

Until now!

Introducing the "Best People Magnet." The Best People Magnet homes in on and harnesses the natural magnetic field around people of excellence. People of excellence emit a slightly different magnetic field than mediocre people. Invisible to the naked eye, the Best People Magnet's highly attuned current will find and attract the right people. Simply turn on the magnet and watch how talented, generous, and well-adjusted individuals flock toward you as if induced into a trance.

Once you have enough people, you can then use the magnet to point them in the direction of your choosing. Do you need an entirely new management team, some extra consultants, a new chairman of the board? Simply point, shoot, and attract. Perhaps you need a date, or you want to find a new doctor, lawyer, or real estate agent. The possibilities are endless.

As an added bonus, we are going to add an additional repeller magnet. To guarantee a new lifestyle, you will also receive the people repeller. Imagine having the ability to ensure any unwanted person who does not meet your criteria will be unable come within 10 feet of you.

If unqualified people enter your zone, the magnetic pulse emitted from the magnet will instantly detain the person by removing all kinetic energy, leaving them paralyzed in place for as long as you like.

You can literally create your own mini-society with you as the beloved leader wherever you go. To attract the best people and free yourself from having to deal with substandard people in all walks of life, order the best people and repeller magnets today.

And every fan of this book will be going home with their very own set of Best People and Repeller magnets. Just look under your chair. It's right there ... congratulations.

Magnetically re-charge your life today.

Finding a New Dream Career and Life Purpose as you Transition through the Stages of Life

Inspired by "Acclaimed Aussie Author," Andrew Griffiths.

What do you do when you lose your dream career? Whether it is due to accident, age, failure, or lack of opportunity to capture it in the first place, your life purpose is likely to change as you progress through many transitions in the stages of life. Living in a world that heavily promotes "right now," it is important to realize that a long and varied life is not only possible, it is a healthy recommendation. No one understands this point better than Australia's #1 selling business author, Andrew Griffiths (pictured above). As a man who lost his dream career at an early age, he has gone on to develop a much greater life purpose and deeper levels of success than he had ever imagined. He states that it is important to see life in chapters that are part of your story but not the entire story. No matter the setback, we can change our life for the better at any stage.

Although it is important to act decisively and be committed to your current purpose, it is also good to know that possible failure does not have to end you. If anything, this should liberate you against the fear of failure, as there is always the possibility of new and enriching success around the next life corner. To help you consider what life is about and maximize future variety and growth regardless of what stage of life you are currently in, the Exploring and Setting the Stages of Life Exercise will be offered after the interview.

In my interview with Andrew, you're going to discover ...

- Bubble in the brain: How he overcame a career-ending injury in order to find a new passion
- **How to capture opportunities to create value and share your expert knowledge effectively**
- The Pretty Woman moment - what he did to transform himself in one night to save his career
- **Embracing transition: What it takes to find happiness through all stages of life**
- Why being decisive is the key to life and career success.

Aleks: Hello, and welcome. I'm Aleks George Srbinoski, founder of **FulfillingHappiness.com**, and today my guest is Andrew Griffiths, who is Australia's number #1 best-selling business author with 11 hugely successful books sold in 50 countries all over the world.

He is an entrepreneur with a real passion for small business. From humble beginnings as an orphan growing up in Western Australia, Andrew has owned and operated a number of very successful small businesses, starting his first enterprise at age seven, a newspaper round in the seedy red-light area of Perth.

Since then he has sold encyclopedias door to door, travelled the world as an international sales manager for a large Japanese shipping company, worked in the Great Sandy Desert for a gold exploration company, had his own SCUBA school and retail shop, and worked as a commercial diver throughout Australia and Papua New Guinea.

His "101 Ways" business-building series offers small business owners practical, smart, and realistic advice. His book, *The Me Myth*, is his first personal growth book and has won acclaim as one of the most inspirational self-improvement books ever written by an Australian author. Known for his ability to entertain, to inspire, and to energize, Andrew has become a highly sought-after keynote speaker. Welcome, Andrew.

Andrew: Hello, Aleks, how are you?

Aleks: I'm very, very well. Really excited to have you with me today.

Andrew: Thank you, I'm excited to be here.

Aleks: Ha, that's right! And this interview will be somewhat about you, not just about me. According to your book, it's not just about me, it's also about others.

Andrew: Absolutely, absolutely, it's a great philosophy, I think.

Aleks: Okay. The question I have for you is, what was the thought process behind the best life-changing decision you have ever made?

Andrew: It's an interesting one, I've had many of those life-changing experiences in my life. Probably the biggest one that's had the most profound effect on my life and where I ended up happened as a result of a pretty serious accident that I had. I used to be a commercial diver, that was what I did as my first kind of real job I guess and my real business, which was I bought a dive shop at the age of 18, and part of that was to be a commercial diver, to recover boats and things like that. Anyway, I was living in Cairns and I was putting in a helicopter pontoon, and I got a case of decompression sickness, which is nitrogen bubbles, which in my case, they were in the brain.

It was really quite a serious situation and quite life-threatening actually, and I ended up having six months of recuperation, and what it really meant was that I couldn't dive anymore. That was a really big thing for me because diving had been a big part of my life and it was always the thing I could fall back on whether commercial or peachin diving or whatever it may have been.

And to all of a sudden be told by a doctor that if you go diving again it probably will kill you, you've got decompression sickness, you maybe end up in a wheelchair or quadriplegic ... the company I was working for at the time was a really big Japanese company and they wanted to do the right thing. It was a workplace kind of accident so they offered me a position in sales and marketing, and I kind of begrudgingly took it.

And that was probably the interesting part, the opportunity was there and I didn't like it. My view was I think I was bitter about the fact that I can't dive anymore, and now I'm being made to go into sales and marketing, and a funny situation evolved Aleks, I ended up in Sydney in a trade show for the tourism industry. My sales and marketing role was promoting tourism, products, cruises for this Japanese company, and I remember being so paranoid about becoming a corporate drone.

To me it was all about I've got to retain my identity and not get lost in this corporate world, and so I refused to wear a suit or anything and I had long hair, beard and earrings, and looked like a typical commercial diver at the time. I was in the trade show with my big boss at the time. This was a huge tradeshow, a big event for the company, and here's my poor CEO and me, a scruffy bum, sitting across the table snarling at anyone who walked by. I remember at the end of the day leaving, and I had this really big realization, quite an epiphany for me, that I had this great opportunity thrown at me to retrain in this whole new industry, a whole new direction, and I buggered it up because when my CEO left, he just shook his head and walked out of the booth for the day and I was thinking, "What have I done?"

And I remember wandering around the streets of Sydney, and the weight and the enormity of my stupidity had dawned on me. I was pretty certain that my boss was going to sack me. I ended up in David Jones (department store), in this really weird situation with this old guy in the suit department. He was just there and he came up to me and said, "You look really sad, is something wrong?" And I told him what happened and said, "I think I've just made the biggest mistake of my life." I explained what happened, and I call it my *"Pretty Woman* moment." Before I know it I'm standing in the floor of David Jones in a chair and this guy had organized someone to cut my hair, a suit, a seamstress to come and hem up the suit, briefcase, the whole thing, I had a complete makeover.

Aleks: (Laughs)

Andrew: At 6 o'clock on a Thursday night in David Jones. Spent a fortune, emptied my entire bank account. And I went back to my hotel, and I remember that night, I hardly slept because I was in this suit and I wanted to stand in front of the mirror and have a look at myself. I had a shave, haircut, it was just hilarious. The next morning I was downstairs at 6 o'clock or something waiting for my boss to come along, and he walked by me several times before he actually recognized me. And then **he saw it was me and said, "What have you done?" It was a complete transformation. We went to the trade show together and that was huge, everything was different, my attitude was different and we sold literally millions of dollars worth of cruises.**

And we were having a drink at the end of the day and my boss said, "Andrew, I came downstairs today to sack you, and to put you on a plane. **I had organized a ticket back for you. I had done all those things and when I saw you and the effort you'd gone to I decided I'm not going to do that. I'll give it a day."** And interestingly enough then, that spurned on everything for me. I ended up working as an international sales manager for this Japanese company, travelled around the world for five years, amazing experiences, started my own marketing company, and of course that led to me writing my first book which then led to me writing another 10 books and getting to where I am today. And **I try to, as often as I can, I give thanks to those nitrogen bubbles because they changed my life wonderfully. It was one of those realizations that right here, right now what's happening is not your entire life, it's just one part of that. It might seem horrible, it might seem terrible right now, but if you give it time and let the situation play out, it's amazing to see what comes, and it's often the best thing that has ever happened to you.**

Aleks: Wow. I wonder if a nitrogen bubble made you make that decision to change your attitude that day (laughs).

Andrew: (laughing) Probably. Absolutely, and it is a funny kind of a thought when you look at it. It's a bit of the *Sliding Doors* kind of concept, which way could you go, which way could your life go, if I go down that path today, what will happen with my life? And I have had a few of those. When I was younger I was going off the beaten track, I was going off the rails, to use a cliché. When I was around 17 and drinking and into drugs and petty crime and stuff and I had the same epiphany. I'm at a crossroads, if I go down this road, my life is very predictable and I'll end up in jail or dead or whatever, and if I go down that road, it's a much more positive and bright future, and I've had maybe three of those kind of epiphanies in my life. They're really powerful and it's nice when they are black and white and you are in control of those incredible decision-making processes.

Aleks: So what do you think would have happened if you didn't do that? If you hadn't made that decision, where you had your Pretty Woman moment? What would've happened if you had rejected the help offered? Did this guy help you in some ways? I wasn't sure about that.

Andrew: What do you mean help me?

Aleks: Did he just offer an ear to listen to or did he actually offer advice or guidance or anything in that realm?

Andrew: Quite a lot of mentorship from that point of view. They didn't just throw me into the sales department and leave me there to flounder and figure it out. Certainly, they walked me through and helped me; it was more like an internship in many respects. I just took to it like a duck to water. I had a big mouth and ended up being pretty good in sales.

Where would I be if I hadn't done that, who knows? I guess like a lot of people I probably would have been lost, I probably would have just floundered around between different industries. I certainly wouldn't have had the opportunities to have done the things that I have done.

There's no doubt about that. Certainly, no doubt in my mind, I wouldn't have become a writer or any of those things. I think it's easy to end up in the grey zone of life and in the shadows in some respects.

Aleks: How did you become an author? Because there still is a bit of a step from being a sales manager to becoming an author and then becoming a prolific author.

Andrew: Again, it's embracing the situation. I had an opportunity. I had a lot of small business clients in my little marketing company. And I realized most of them all shared really similar problems and they were all problems that I had experienced having run my own businesses for most of my working life. It was interesting, they would come in and it was the same spiel. It's the same today, they had common issues and common problems. And they couldn't afford, back then anyway, they couldn't really afford a marketing consultant.

I started writing a series of fax sheets. People would ring me and say, "Hey, I need more business" or "I need to make a brochure" or "I need this" or "I need that," and I could literally fax it to them. **Not a very good business move, giving everything away for free, but it was a way to help people, and contribution is a big part of my world and who I am. And one day I realized wow, I've got 50 of these fact sheets, maybe if I write another 50, there's 100, and I could write a book, 101 ways to market your business. I spoke to quite a few people in the industry at the time and pretty much all of them said, "Don't do it, no one is going to publish a book on marketing. And who are you to write a book on marketing?" I've got some good friends! And interesting enough because all that did is make me want to do it even more.**

I did my homework, found a friend, she worked in a publishing company and I sent the initial manuscript to her boss. They didn't like it; it wasn't their direction at the time, but that lady knew another lady who worked at Allen & Unwin and she asked me if I minded if they send it across to her. And they did. And I was contacted by Allen & Unwin straight away and they said, "We love it, we want to publish it." And the first book sold really well and they said, "Have you got anymore?" and I said, "Absolutely!"

And I worked my way through all of the aspects of small business, customer service, how to sell stuff, how to advertise, how to have a business and a life. All of those kinds of topics, and next thing I know those are all the books that are out and they've all sold really well.

Again, a little bit of circumstance, but **I could have listened to what people said and not done it out of fear of rejection as well, and I think that's a big thing. A lot of people out there, everyone wants to write a book, but if you want to write a book, you've actually got to write a book. That tends to be a bit of a stumbling block for a lot of people. It's interesting now to be Australia's #1 business author. I haven't got any real business training or business education, which is ironic in some respects. So if I can become that person that shows it, there's plenty of opportunity for everyone.**

Aleks: I'd just like to ask, we're wrapping up now, what would you advise to someone who faces a situation you have faced? Where they were in a place where they weren't happy, their life had to change, and they have to make a decision. What would you say to them to encourage them? What would be your *Pretty Woman* moment for them?

Andrew: I think the first part about it is procrastination is a bit of a killer. **If you're not careful you can procrastinate away for the next 10-20 years. And I think that happens a lot of the time. It reaches a point where you literally just have to make a decision. And that is actually what forces your hand. Is there a right or wrong decision to be made? It's more about just making a decision and getting on with your life rather than living in the limbo side of things.**

I think the other part of that, my take on it is, **whatever is happening right here, right now, is just one chapter in your life; it's not the entire book. But what you do right now is going to have a pretty dramatic effect on which direction your life takes, the outcome of your book, or the ending of your book. So make the decision, understand that right here, right now is just part of the journey, it's not the whole journey, and be open to that fact.**

I've seen so much evidence of this in my life and with the people I know and work with and care for, and all those kind of things. Once you actually make that decision to go down a certain path, if it's the right path doors start to open. If it's the wrong path you get signs saying it's the wrong path, so it becomes quite clear, I think.

Aleks: Fantastic. Thank you so much for your time today. Finally, where can people find out more about you, Andrew?

Andrew: Just go to my website: **www.AndrewGriffiths.com.au**. Plenty of information there, plenty of details, some free stuff, some sample chapters from books, and a blog there, as well, with a pile of info on it. Thank you.

Aleks: Thank you.

Exploring and Setting the Stages of Life Exercise

In exploring the stages of life, I have found that a good number to use is seven. So you will be breaking up your life into age groups of seven. Zero-7, 7-14, 14-21, 21-28, 28-35, 35-42 and so on up to 84 or more if you like.

1. Clear the mind - Sit or stand straight with your shoulders back and head up. You can either close your eyes or have them open, but look slightly up and take three deep breaths. With each breath, clear your mind by focusing all your attention on your breath.

This will ground you into the present moment and open your mind.

Continue to relax and breathe deeply as we go through this exercise now if it is safe to do so, or later when you are in the right environment to proceed.

2. Imagine you are in a cinema with a large screen projecting in front of you. On the screen you are going to envision and experience your ideal life from beginning to end. At each stage you experience you are going to absorb the lessons and notice how you change and grow through each stage.

3. a) Go back and watch yourself go through an ideal life period between the ages of 0-7. Just notice life in terms of snapshots, short scenes, and magic moments. Really notice how you see your ideal world at this age, how you hear it, smell, and taste it and how it feels overall.

Notice how you grow and change, and absorb the lessons from this experience.

b) Now watch yourself go through an ideal life period between the ages of 7-14. Just notice life in terms of snapshots, short scenes, and magic moments. Really notice how you see your ideal world at this age, how you hear it, smell, and taste it and how it feels overall.

Notice how you grow, change, and live differently as you absorb the lessons from this experience.

c) Now watch yourself go through an ideal life period between the ages of 14-21. Just notice life in terms of snapshots, short scenes, and magic moments. Really notice how you see your ideal world at this age, how you hear it, smell, and taste it and how it feels overall.

Notice how you grow, change, and live differently as you absorb the lessons from this experience.

d) If possible at this time, continue with this process all the way through exploring every seven-year period up until the right point for you. If it's not possible to do this right now, choose a time to start again, and complete the rest of this process later.

Once completed, write down what you experienced and learned from each stage and how you will use that experience to better shape your own future and those of others important to you.

Fantasy Gift – Minor Mentor Mind Shaping Ear-Piece

Feeling lost, confused, and uncertain about your life and which direction to take? Knowing that there are so many paths, twists, and turns ahead of you, it's not surprising that it can all get a little too overwhelming. If only you had a guide, someone who has been there, done that and is now ready to lead you step-by-step with safety and assurance straight to the promised land.

Wouldn't it be great if you had someone in your head, an expert who could just take all that indecision away and just tell you what to do? Someone with the perfect voice, a voice that both soothes and inspires you, a voice that is direct and dedicated to your success every minute of every day. A guiding voice that does not need to sleep, never ages, and is always right!

Well, that voice exists and it is ready to penetrate deeply into your mind … it's time to change your life!

Introducing the "Mini-Mentor Mind Shaper Ear-Piece." Specifically designed to fit neatly within any ear, this mini miracle of mind engineering and communications technology will finally set you on the right path. Forget those antiquated rules of being. A life of trial and error, self-discovery, trials and tribulations is no longer wanted or necessary.

Made with real human skin and utilizing the world's smallest and most powerful microchip, the Mini-Mentor fits seamlessly into any ear cavity and soothes the mind by altering brain waves for the task at hand while at the same time producing empowering action commands created by the world's most successful people that are sure to inspire and energize.

You never need to be uncertain again! Imagine a life without confusion, a world of clear paths and blue skies supported by an endless inner stream of empowered thoughts, feelings, and actions.

Well, now you can live in that world!

You no longer need to worry about your future, as you will always be guided ... there is always going to be that voice in your ear that's there for you.

It's time to finally let go to take control. Order the Mini-Mentor Mind Shaping ear piece today and get ready to sing along to a brand new song.

And every fan of this book will be going home with their very own Mini-Mentor Mind Shaper ear piece. Just look under your chair. It's right there ... congratulations.

The Mini-Mentor Mind Shaper. An ear-full of intelligence.

Establishing Personal, Social, and Public Accountability Practices to Achieve your Goals and Enhance Leadership Skills

Inspired by the "Passionate Persuader," John G. Miller.

The reality is most of the goals we set in life will not come to fruition. However, by developing personal, social, and public accountability procedures around those of the most importance, high-level success is possible. There really only appears to be two reasons why you will not achieve your goals. It was either because the goal was not emotionally compelling enough to begin with, or because of a lack of accountability measures.

Best-selling business author John G. Miller (pictured above) knows just how crucial accountability is. His own personal and business mission is simply "Helping organizations and people be outstanding through personal accountability!" Accountability is also the essential ingredient for the development of future leadership skills and abilities.

Creating a new standard of being is perhaps the hardest enterprise we personally and professionally face. Fortunately, knowing how to create the right kind of pressure can continuously push you into the right direction. To help you raise your standards and reach your goals, after the interview you will be exposed to the 4 Ps of A-level Accountability.

In my interview with John, you're going to discover ...

- His amazing role reversal: What he did to excel under his mentor and eventually become his boss
- **How to present yourself in a way that builds trust and respect, even when you have no career-related experience**
- "Believe ..." – The simple mantra John hires, fires, and lives by
- **Why following your "gut" is the best way to find and advance your career and life**
- The importance of being energetic and fully connecting with others if you want to be a superior salesperson.

Aleks: Hello, and welcome. My name is Aleks George Srbinoski, founder of **FufillingHappiness.com.** Today, my guest is author and speaker, John G. Miller. John has a clear mission: "Helping Organizations and People Be Outstanding Through Personal Accountability!" He is the author of the best-selling books, *QBQ! The Question Behind the Question* and *Flipping the Switch*, as well as *Outstanding! 47 Ways to Make Your Organization Exceptional!* John lives near Denver, Colorado with his wife of 31 years, Karen, and they together co-authored the book *Parenting the QBQ Way.* They have seven children and one grandson, which sounds pretty accountable to me. So first of all, hello, John.

John: Aleks, thank you for having me on today.

Aleks: You are more than welcome. I am here to ask you a really big question ...

John: All right.

Aleks: ...and the question is what was the thought process behind the best life-changing decision you have ever made?

John: All right, well that's probably one of the easiest questions I've ever been asked. First of all, I need to put the disclaimer in, are you saying the best decision after the decision to marry my wife Karen, Aleks? Is that what you're saying? (laughs)

Aleks: (Laughing) It's really up to you how you want to answer that question; it can go either way. (laughs)

John: Well, I just wanted to say that the best decision was marrying Karen.

Aleks: Sure.

John: The next best decision was driven not by a conscious thought process; it was driven by intense boredom.

Aleks: Ah ha ...

John: I came out of Cornell University in 1980 and Karen and I got married – she was 19 and I was 22. We moved to the Midwest because I had gotten a job with a big company, and I started doing work for that big company. I was actually a grain trader. It sounds exciting but it was not. I would buy and sell corn, soy beans, wheat, and oats but basically it meant sitting at a desk and calling farmers and what's called "country elevators" and telling them my price for corn that day and seeing if they wanted to sell any. I can remember, Aleks, just months ... months into my career with this big company after coming out of Cornell, an Ivy League Institution and all, my wife wrote in her journal, "John is bored."

I mean, I had just started my career in August of 1980 and by October of 1980 she is writing "John is bored," and we looked back at that and say, "Yep, and I was." I stayed five more years.

You know, I was kind of in the trance. I thought I had to work for the big company, spend 30 years there, get a gold watch, retire. We ended up moving to several cities: Southern Minnesota, Montana, Missouri, over to Minneapolis.

One day it struck me that I didn't have to do this. I didn't have to stay at this desk; I didn't have to work for this company. Basically, what happened was a friend said to me, quote, "If you don't like your life why don't you change it?" And I probably said something like, "Really, you mean I'm in control, I'm accountable, I own my decisions?" And so within months I started interviewing and looking for a sales career because someone had said, "You should get into sales," and nobody in my family had been formerly in sales but this person said, "You should get into sales, you've got that kind of personality." So, I started interviewing with big companies, through head hunters, and search firms, and one day I opened the Minneapolis newspaper up and there was an ad there, Aleks, that said **"WANTED: High Energy Successful Salesperson To Sell Training." I remember flying down the stairs to a typewriter and wanting to type a letter to the company and my wife said, "You can't apply to that, you've never sold before," and I said, "But I have high energy!"**(laughs)

I flew down the stairs and typed out a letter that I still have today, if you can believe it, because the boss who eventually hired me eventually gave it to me and it had two typos in it. **He interviewed 15 people, he got 60 resumes, he interviewed 15 people and there was something, Aleks, about me. He told me years later it was my energy. It was me sitting on the edge of the couch, leaning forward, it was me saying, "Well, I don't know if I'd like to cold call but I'm happy to try it." So, he saw a risk-taker and he hired me to sell leadership and management training, and I did that for the next decade.** I actually did become #1 salesperson the last five years I was there. Then, I went off in 1995 to go on my own to be an author and a speaker. But it was all really driven, Aleks, by boredom, and clearly the boredom had a foundation.

I was not in a job that was suited for me; I wasn't designed or wired to sit at a desk. I found my passion a few years later when I got this job selling training in Minneapolis, St. Paul. I was driving around the Twin Cities every day, going on appointments, calling on executives, persuading, selling, offering ideas, pursuing, and following up.

Plus, I was moving – physically moving all day long. I was driving to an 8 a.m. appointment there, a 10 a.m. appointment there. It was just the total opposite of working at a desk from 8 to 5, 8 to 5.

Plus, I didn't have a boss looking over my shoulder and looking at his watch if I wasn't at my desk at 8 a.m. and left before 5 p.m. **I had become my own boss. Back then, in 1986, I didn't know I was so entrepreneurial and such a risk-taker, but it turned out that was how I was wired. Now here I am, all these years later, still self-employed, loving what I do. So, that's what really drove it: I was bored because I was in the wrong job.**

Aleks: Fantastic, fantastic. So you've mentioned a couple really interesting things I just want to pick up on. The first thing you mentioned was how your attitude above all else allowed you to make that leap. It allowed you to emotionally impact who would become your boss because he felt something in you and he just had to hire you.

John: Yes, he told me years later ... by the way, this is one of those circle of life ideas, he now sells QBQ Personal Accountability Training for me. He is 10 years older than I am, he's in his 60s now I'm in my 50s, and he actually sells my training.

Aleks: (laughs)

John: Yeah, isn't that a great story? He's the guy that brought me into the business in 1986. I was 28 and he was 38, and he told me later that **he had interviewed other people that had more sales experience but he hadn't seen that kind of innate energy and drive in the other people. It was really a gut call, and that's what happens when you hire people sometimes. It's a gut call, it's not a science.** We can't put them under a microscope and know whether they will succeed or not but there was something in my attitude, the way I was thinking, my physicality.

Again, he was a master at interviews; he was a tall man so he sat in the tall back chair and I'm a shorter guy and he sat me on the couch and most people slump into the couch, most people, **they sink into it**

and really lose their power and he will tell you that I got out of the cushions and sat on the edge of the couch leaning forward, and he just sensed I was someone who could call on executives and sell training and so he hired me and you know, I was off to the races. I had quite honestly ... You asked why did I make this decision and one thing that I didn't know at that time, Aleks, is that I didn't have a mentor.

I didn't have a coach. I didn't have somebody who had intense belief in me and wanted me to succeed. At the big company, I just had a collection of managers who weren't very good, they didn't train and coach. Nobody really seemed to care. **I needed to take accountability for my own development and so I went out and found a mentor, and this guy spent the next 10 years training me to speak, training me to facilitate, training me to sell training. He taught me so much, and here I am many years later still using everything he taught me. Again, now he represents our company.**

Aleks: Oh that's wonderful. That's such a fantastic story. We are coming to the end of our time, incredibly there is so much more I could ask. What I'd like to just end off with is what advice would you give to other people who have to make that tough decision?

John: Absolutely, as we say in all my material, I have a favorite meeting theme. **Believe or leave. Believe or leave. If you do not believe in the organization you represent, if you do not believe in the products and services they provide, if you do not believe in your colleagues, your team, your boss. If you are struggling with your belief in self, it's time to get out. Life is too short to have a mission statement that says, "I owe, I owe, so off to work I go."** That's a terrible way to live. I don't want to live for Friday.

I want to love what I do so if I don't believe anymore, it's time to go out and find something to do that I believe in. Then, what happens is my Fridays become my Mondays, and my Mondays become my Fridays. Then, the work weeks are exciting and I'm not waiting for the weekend. Believe or leave, that's my advice to anybody.

Aleks: Well, I believe you! I definitely believe you there.

John: (laughs)

Aleks: Well now that's fantastic, and I thank you so much for your time. Where can people find out more about you, John?

John: Thanks for asking, Aleks. **QBQ.com** and that stands for the Question Behind the Question, very simple. QBQ.com and they can find out all about us there.

Aleks: Excellent, thank you so much for being part of this series.

John: Thanks for having me on, Aleks.

4 Ps of A-level Accountability

Here are the 4 Ps of accountability and some quick strategies on how to best incorporate each of the principles. Be aware that they are in ascending level of power. In other words, the 4th P is the highest level of accountability, but all 4 are beneficial and work best when all utilized together.

The 4 Ps are:

Personal accountability

Partner accountability

Party accountability

Public accountability

The first person you have to be accountable to is "you." As part of this stage you are to get clear on your compelling reasons for pursuing the goal and write out a list of the benefits of obtaining the goal and consequences of not obtaining it. Then narrow the list to the top 5 most emotionally intense benefits and consequences.

Place the list in a highly visible place or in multiple places and review frequently.

To enhance personal accountability, consider crafting a mission statement, creating a scrapbook with relevant images, journaling on your commitment, and developing a set of beliefs, rules, and expectations that you verbally declare to follow through on a regular basis. Put as many positive reminders of the goal in your environment as possible.

The next level up is becoming accountable to a "partner." Being vulnerable and declaring your goals in front of another person is difficult.

What you want at this level is someone who is supportive, trustworthy, positive, but also firm. Your partner CAN NOT be an "it's okay" kind of person. You have to hate the idea of disappointing them, as they will not be accepting of any run-of-the-mill excuses.

Checking in on a regular basis, preferably daily, is best and to enhance the process, making friendly bets should be incorporated. The bet should offer a nice reward if you succeed and a reasonably annoying and irritating consequence if you do not. For example, if you are successful, your partner takes you out to your favourite restaurant, but if you fail you have to wash their car every week for a month.

The next level is to be accountable to a "party." Having not just one person but a group of people you are committed to will add support and usually increase compliance. Especially if you are in the right kind of group who all share similar beliefs, attitudes and are determined to succeed. Everything you do with a partner you can also do with a group, but now you are committed to more people.

The highest level of accountability is "public." This is where you do everything you can to tell everyone about your goal. Everyone you meet should know about it. It should be revealed across websites and social media channels, and questions from whomever must be encouraged and welcomed. You should brand yourself with your goal, perhaps making T-shirts and other paraphernalia related to it. At this level, it may even become a cause.

You may notice that this is what many celebrities will do if they have really struggled with a certain goal, usually weight loss. They will declare it publicly through the media and advertising. With so many people now aware of the goal, the potential pain and embarrassment for not succeeding is very high, but also the potential support and pleasure for succeeding is magnified many times over. Another example of accountability at this level is entering competitions or starting goal-related groups. When you go public, you have the opportunity to be a role-model and make a real positive social impact.

Success at this level is guaranteed to increase self-esteem, confidence, and pride. Even if only a few people learn of and actively support your efforts, your frequent public declarations show just how serious and committed you are.

Those are the 4 Ps. Ideally, you want to have all 4 levels catered to. Consider a goal you currently have and work through this process.

Fantasy Gift – The Self-Esteemer

Let's face it: reaching your goals and fulfilling your potential is not usually an easy thing. Life is filled with roadblocks and challenges. Life is hard, but who says it has to be that way? Your experiences are all about your perceptions, and what you believe becomes your reality.

But learning to be positive is no walk in the park, and based on current obesity rates not many people are doing that anyway. If you want to reach your goals you need to believe in yourself, but who wants to do all that heavy lifting? I know I don't.

Well now you don't have to either. Introducing "The Self-Esteemer." The Self-Esteemer uses Swedish vapor technology to help you sweat out all the negative beliefs and toxins in your brain and body, leaving only pure and positive thoughts, beliefs, and body-chemistry. All you have to do is sit, relax, put on a little music, and let the Self-Esteemer do all the work. We all know it's not your fault you've become a little plump around the edges and a little less confident in recent years. Hey, it's okay, it's okay, my friend; that's why the Self-Esteemer was created.

As your body and brain begin to change, you may notice other people around you starting to ask questions. You may hear them say, "You don't seem to do anything; how could you suddenly be so trim and positive?" Well, don't hold back –let them know! Ask them to join you, as the Self-Esteemer can cater to up to eight people. Why not relax and take it easy with your new Self-Esteemer group?

Now the big question we get is, "Should I go for a walk within 24 hours of my daily steams?" You'll be pleased to know that you won't need to walk anymore. In fact, it is advised that you move as little as possible and drive frequently. The last thing you want to do is feel the negative and toxic effects of exertion-based sweat.

As for food, that's right, you can eat whatever you want, as the heat from the steam removes non-essential ingredients of food without sacrificing taste. Now, what about children, is it safe for them? Absolutely, get them away from those dangerous and dirty neighborhood parks and back inside where they belong.

As an added bonus, we are going to give away a set of steam-free screen protectors. That way you'll be able to watch TV, and the children can play their video games as you all feel the incredible lifestyle benefits of the Self-Esteemer.

To finally be the highly respectable person you deserve to be without any effort at all, order the Self-Esteemer today.

And every fan of this book will be going home with their very own Self-Esteemer. Just look under your chair. It's right there ... congratulations.

The Self-Esteemer. Feel that self-esteem rising!

Have you Told Your Inner and/or Outer Circle about this Book?

If you have told others about it, thank you, I really appreciate it.

If you have not and you are able to do so, that would be really great!

As I said, the life of a "solo entrepreneur" can be harsh and finding supportive and likeminded people is essential. We don't have large marketing budgets, major publishing contacts, PR teams or established bookselling contracts.

What we do have is a lot of hours behind a computer and a dream of sharing the value in our creations.

What I value and rely on most, is one very special relationship and that is the one I have with you, my reader.

Please mention the book to your colleagues, friends and family and of course visit my site and use your social media networks to let others know as well. If possible, leaving a review at the place you obtained the book (e.g. Amazon.com) would be great as well.

Whatever you decide, thank you in advance for reading this far and may you use what you have learnt to forge a greater destiny.

P.S. As a thank you, I'm sending you my next Fantasy Gift Prototype – The Circle of Influence Generator. Similar to hula-hoops, you throw these circles around important people and they instantly become followers and part of your inner circle. It's in the imaginary post as we speak.

When they get the book, they too will get the extra goodies at:
FulfillingHappiness.com/dddbonuses

Becoming an Industry Leader through Business Creativity, Innovation, and Entrepreneurship

With the "Learned Leader," Randy Komisar.

It would be hard to deny the fact that we are living in the world of specialization. To the detriment of business creativity, innovation, and entrepreneurship, many people are taught and expected to only become highly knowledgeable in their specific areas of work. However, many revolutionary industry leaders are cross-trainers.

Cross-trainers in the sense that they have active knowledge and study of numerous fields and find ways to creatively incorporate and cross-pollinate what they know. Thereby creating something far superior than what would have existed if they were focused on their own field and specialization only.

As a Silicon Valley entrepreneur and previous CEO of several major technology companies, Randy Komisar (pictured above) understands the importance of developing and challenging himself fully. He claims that the greatest creative satisfaction comes from being a keen business generalist. He has been a writer, teacher, speaker, investor, businesses builder, as well as the inventor of new roles and industries.

Success and fulfilment truly do appear to arise from the cultivation of the creative self. After all, how satisfying and stimulating is it to work on and promote already well-established ideas and technologies? It does not matter if you are referring to your industry or the development of yourself. Knowing how to tap into your own previous training and experiences and use that knowledge to create at a higher innovative level is what you will be learning today with a simple 5-step creativity cross-training exercise and checklist, to be delivered after the interview.

In my interview with Randy, you're going to discover ...

- How to avoid the personal growth-destroying temptation to seek safe career paths and positions
- **"Renaissance man": What it takes to develop all the roles and abilities inside yourself**
- How to leap before you look – how one secret discussion in a darkroom led him to pursue a completely different career.
- **The expansive mindset that led him to overcome his original reluctance to write**
- Why he rejected major opportunities to be a high level specialist with numerous firms in order to pursue his deeper needs.

Aleks: Hello, and welcome. I'm Aleks George Srbinoski, founder of **FulfillingHappiness.com** and today my guest is Randy Komisar, who joined a world-leading venture capital firm located in the Silicon Valley, Kleiner Perkins Caufield & Byers in 2005 as a partner. For several years prior, Randy worked with entrepreneurs creating businesses with leading-edge technologies.

He was a co-founder of Claris Corporation, served as CEO for Lucas Arts Entertainment and Crystal Dynamics, and acted as a "virtual CEO" for such companies as WebTV and GlobalGiving. He is a founding director of TiVo and serves on the Global Advisory Board for the UCSB Institute for Energy Efficiency. Earlier, Randy served as CFO of GO Corporation and Senior Counsel for Apple Computer, following a private practice in Technology Law.

Randy holds a BA in Economics from Brown University and a JD from Harvard Law School. He is a lecturer on entrepreneurship at Stanford University and author of the best-selling book *The Monk and the Riddle*, as well as several articles on leadership and entrepreneurship. He is also the co-author of a new book on managing innovation, *Getting to Plan B*. First of all, welcome, Randy.

Randy: Oh, thank you, Aleks.

Aleks: Thank you so much for joining me today. I really appreciate it, and I can't wait to hear about your progressive ideas. So let's dive right in. The first question I always ask is, what was the thought process behind the best life-changing decision you have ever made?

Randy: (laughs). That's a good question. Most of the significant life-changing decisions I have made have been relatively thoughtless. I thought it would be interesting to talk about two of them because they sort of indicate the way in which I approach these questions.

When I was a youngster at Apple computer, I was approached by a fellow by the name of Bill Campbell to spin out a software company called Claris Corporation. And at that time, it was just Apple software; we hadn't actually named it, and I was the first person he came to. I was sort of walking down the hall one day at Apple. I did not know Bill that well. We had come in contact in doing some various deals since I was a lawyer at Apple and he was Vice President, Executive Vice President of Sales.

He grabbed me one day, pulled me into a darkroom, literally, sat me down and told me he was about to spin out the software assets of Apple. And he was going to be the founder and he was looking for a co-founder, and was I in or was I out? And the interesting thing about that was I knew nothing about what he was about to do. He didn't offer me a job. There was no job title involved. He didn't talk about compensation. I knew nothing about my ownership position or what my actual role responsibilities were.

But it was quite clear that this guy was giving me a chance of a lifetime across the table in the dark, and … I just jumped at it. **And I think the reason I jumped at it, the process that was going through my mind at that time was how unique the opportunity was. This was a man who had a great reputation. It was a chance to move from being a lawyer to being a businessman. It was a chance to learn to be an entrepreneur. And it was the chance to grow,** and so I left a perfectly great job with a career ahead of me in law to join Bill Campbell in founding Claris Corporation.

I later worked with Bill when I went to GO Corporation and was the CFO for Bill. I later left Bill, left GO Corporation, and Bill was my chief reference and sponsor when I got my first CEO job at Lucas Arts Entertainment for George Lucas. **And I realized that in making that leap, I created a friendship and the mentorship of a lifetime.**

I want to fast forward, though, to the next stage of my career. I became a CEO in large part because my mentor Bill Campbell believed I was capable of doing it. I wasn't highly motivated or driven to be the leader. I was very interested more in the process; I like doing good work. I like interesting problems; being the boss was never my goal.

But he encouraged me to do it, saw my abilities there, and I went in as a CEO first for Lucas Arts Entertainment and then later for a company called Crystal Dynamics and another game company actually financed by this group that I am with today, Kleiner Perkins Caufield & Byers.

I realized one year into that how miserable I was. The company was doing fine. It wasn't great, it wasn't bad. I had a very good team around me, the products were well received, and I was really unhappy.

And I made one of the hardest decisions probably of my life at that point, which was to jump out of a perfectly good airplane and free fall without a job, turning my back on a career as CEO, which I believed was going to lead to a succession of larger and larger companies. And to go off and re-create myself into something called a Virtual CEO. The reason I did that was I wanted to get back in touch with my creative self and get out of the conventional expectations that were surrounding me and my career path.

And so once again, I sort of made this leap without knowing what was ahead of me, but only knowing what was behind me. I knew the certainty and I didn't know the uncertainty, and I leapt into the void and the rest is history. And of course after that, I did that for a number of companies, WebTV and TiVo. I wrote my first book, which was well received, taught at Stanford for a while, wrote a second book, worked with several social ventures and now here as a partner of Kleiner Perkins Caufield & Byers.

So I think that **decision process is pretty consistent for me. It's making these leaps of faith and avoiding the conventional path, in particular the known path for the opportunities of the unknown.**

Aleks: And is that something that you still continue to do now? Is that part of how you approach your work at this point?

Randy: It is, Aleks. It is interesting because the nature of what I do today is to make these leaps and to do it as part of investing in others, in these entrepreneurs who I then put money into, but more importantly roll up my sleeves and help to create, businesses and to see their vision have impact in the marketplace. So I live in this world of uncertainty and ambiguity … this place where I am very, very comfortable. And that sort of is my milieu.

When I first left the law firm, my last law firm, to join Apple computers some 25 years ago, I can remember a similar process where Apple had asked me to leave the law firm and join Apple. But it was very déclassé for a "firm" lawyer to leave to join a company at that stage. But I remember walking down the hall one day and looking, seeing the junior partners and the senior partners and the managing partners' offices all down the row and realizing that was my future; and immediately deciding right then that it was time to leave.

Aleks: Okay. So what do you think would have happened if you hadn't made that decision?

Randy: I think I would have continued on a conventional path that probably would have continued to **bring me some success, maybe significant financial success and notoriety, and maybe not. There's a lot of that that's out of your control, but I think I would have missed an awful lot, what has unfolded for me as I exercised my creative self, and as I invested more in others than I would have been investing in my own success. There's a great reward in that and so I have been able to try different parts of myself … to write, to teach, to speak, to invest, to help others build businesses, to invent new roles, to invent new industries.**

Those opportunities I would never have had, had I stayed on lawyer row or had I stayed at Apple computer. Even if I've stayed at Crystal Dynamics as a CEO, moving on to my next bigger CEO role.

Aleks: Sorry you caught my attention when you said "lawyer row."

Randy: (laughs) That's how I remember it.

Aleks: (laughs) Right, yeah. Who's the criminal here? I'm just wondering.

Randy: (laughs)

Aleks: Okay, so what you are saying is because of this decision you've actually had a much, much more varied life. Is that what you are saying?

Randy: It's been richer and **I've been able to discover more sides of me. I think it's pretty easy for us to assume we are exactly who we seem to be at that moment, that our skill sets are what they appear to be at that moment, that our personality traits are exactly what's being expressed at the moment. That we define ourselves by who we see in the mirror versus by our potential, and I just always feel too constrained by any particular set of definitions.** It's not popular to be a Renaissance person in the day and age of specialization, but I have always admired Renaissance people.

And, yes, there's this slight disappointment in never being completely excellent, the number one in any particular field but there's a reward of sampling and trying so many different things that the trade off to me is pretty straightforward. I always favor leaping into the abyss.

Aleks: Wow, that's fantastic. I mean one of the things I teach is this idea that we have different personas and we have different aspects of our personality, and all of those aspects need to be fed to a certain extent. Without that, you don't really have the richest life that you can have; you won't have as much fulfilling happiness as you can. I think that's what you're saying, is that by exploring these different options and just going for it in all these different ways, you are able to have a richness of life that you never would have dreamed possible before.

Randy: Well, it's interesting because when I wrote my first book, *The Monk and the Riddle*, Harvard Press had actually come out to Silicon Valley to speak with me, and my office was in a coffee shop. I decided when I left Corporate America, I wanted to have an office in a coffee shop. For eight years I had my office in the coffee shop, and it was wonderful. And so they visit me in the coffee shop and they sat down and they said, "You know, we think you have some interesting points of view, we've read a little about you, we know a little about your career, would you be interested writing a book?"

My immediate response was, "No, I'm not a writer." I don't have a story in my head, I don't have any real wisdom to relate, and I don't really know how to write. And so I kindly thanked them and then went off that night to think about it. When I woke up the next morning the thought that jumped into my head was, nobody's ever going ask me to write a book again. This door is open once, it's a great door, walk through it, see what's on the other side, and I did. And *The Monk and the Riddle* was on the other side. And as hard a process as that was, the satisfaction of having done it was something I never would have experienced otherwise.

Aleks: That's fantastic! Well, Randy, it has been an absolute pleasure having you speak with me. So where can people find out more about you?

Randy: Well, you know, I actually keep a relatively low profile. I don't have a web page. I'm not on Facebook. You can find me though at Kleiner Perkins Caufield & Byers.com or **kpcb.com**.

That's probably the best way to reach out if you are interested, but you can also explore my books. You can look me up on Google and there are a lot of lectures that I have done and talks, and so if you are interested in sorts of things that I have done and my point of view, you can get more of it online.

Aleks: That's fantastic! Thank you very much.

Randy: Thank you, Aleks.

Creativity Cross-Training Exercise

With creativity cross-training, it is important to realize that the principles you learn in one field, if intelligently applied, relate the enhancement and originality of who you become in other fields.

Here is a simple 5-step step checklist process to help you discover and develop your creativity cross-training abilities.

1. **Create a list of all the creative activities you find enjoyable.** If you struggle to create a list of at least 10, do an internet search of lists of creative activities related to Music, Art, Design, Writing, Sports, Crafts, Computing, Engineering, Hobbies, Drama, and Dance and anything else you can think of, and tick off ones of interest.

2. **Review your past and childhood.** List all the activities you used to enjoy in the past. Go right back into your childhood and explore old creative works if you still have them.

3. **Consider your current and previous interests and ask yourself how much do you enjoy these activities and why?**

4. **Create a list of online sites about creativity and local places in your area that could trigger ideas.** Consider museums, festivals, shows, open nights, particular interest groups, and so on. Also consider talking to creative friends and generating ideas from them and schedule visits to such places.

5. **Decide on a new creative pursuit, or develop enhancements to an existing creative pursuit and answer: how can I apply in three new ways the skills developed from this creative pursuit to improve my daily life and/or in relation to a specific project?**

For example: If you decide to take acting classes, how could you use what you learn to interact better with clients, control emotions, or improve preparation for certain career transitions and roles?

If exploring art, consider such things as: how could I improve the design of my reports, improve my work or home environment and add more color, flair, and originality to my wardrobe?

Fantasy Gift - Creativity Cross-Trainers

Creativity! We are born as creative beings, but many will die as shells of their true potential. Even though creativity is celebrated, finding the key to it seems to remain a mystery. How do we access this incredible energy that lies hidden within us? How do we find it, control it, and direct it? Perhaps looking for straight answers in the brain alone is not the way to go.

Maybe ... the answer rests deep inside our soles.

Great creative acts are highly physical. Music, drama, art, and of course, dance. At the base of our creative physical selves are our feet. To finally be able to freely access your creative self and step ahead of the pack, you are going to need to develop a different rhythm and a better stride. What if creativity really does come from our soles?

Introducing the "Creativity Cross-Trainers." The ultimate leap forward. Forget classes and countless hours of disciplined practice and refinement. All you really need is the right pair of shoes. Cinderella, Dorothy, and Michael Jordan all attribute their greatest successes to having the right shoes. The Creativity Cross-Trainers are designed to work with any wardrobe and occasion and change color, shape, and density as required.

Because the feet are the furthest away from the brain, we tend to lose most of our creative energy by the time we take our steps. However, the cross-trainers have hundreds of sensors in each sole that amplify the speed and strength of signals between the feet and brain. The result is many more bursts of creative energy reach the feet, and the natural perpetual motion of your feet maintain that energy and circulate it back through your entire body. In simple terms, these cross-trainers create happy feet!

Happy feet lead to the ultimate life experiences. You're about to discover Hollywood's and Broadway's biggest musical secret. Have you ever wondered how musicians, actors, artists, singers, and dancers seem to spontaneously find rhythm and synchronicity time after time, performance after performance? It's the shoes.

If you want a rich, melodic life, if you want to sing the high notes, dance the quick steps, and spontaneously burst into exquisitely choreographed song and dance sequences in unison with complete strangers, these cross-trainers are for you. No matter the challenge and no matter the context, a pain-free and dynamic sole-ution awaits. Order the Creativity Cross-Trainers and put your best foot forward today.

And every fan of this book will be going home with their very own pair of creativity cross trainers. Just look under your chair. They're right there ... congratulations.

The Creativity Cross-Trainers. Now you got sole.

Start-Up the Right Way:

10 Guidelines for

Entrepreneurial Happiness

Now for the key "happiness" message. This is the part of the book where I say, "you now have the power", and "you can be anything you want", and "success is waiting for you." Not quite! What I guarantee instead is: You're going to have failures. You're going to face rejection. You're going to lose money on fruitless ideas and campaigns. I tell you this not to scare you, but to strengthen your resolve. My belief is your psychological health must always be your first priority.

Starting a business is one of the riskiest things you can ever do. The odds of success are against you and there is much to learn. As an entrepreneurial psychologist, I feel it is my responsibility to be as honest and protective as I can. That is why before I reveal the passions-based business model, I sincerely advise you to diligently review and apply the Entrepreneurial Happiness (E-HAPPINESS) guidelines to your business and personal life.

Remember: Happiness is the key to success and not vice versa. Developing happiness-focused beliefs and habits will give you the strength, the patience, and the fortitude to move through the very real obstacles you must overcome on your path to freedom.

The E-HAPPINESS Guidelines

Entry and Exit Limits: Set strict entry and exit goals and budgets. My belief is, "follow your dreams, but always with a plan of how you will cover your responsibilities." If you have children, your financial responsibilities are significantly greater than for someone who does not. You have three start-up business options. Work full time and build your business when not at work, work part-time so you have more hours to commit, or quit all employment. Whatever you decide, it is never wise to risk it all and throw caution to the wind to follow your passion. Always create a plan.

Personally, I think maintaining full time employment is the option least likely to lead to business success, due to fatigue and lack of time. Working part time in an attempt to maintain your basic financial responsibilities is a good option as long as you remain committed on your goal outside of those work hours to build your business. Quitting all employment is a good option only if you already have a good understanding, training and contacts in that industry and you have a strict business plan and timeframe with all basic expenses covered for the timeframe.

For example, you may need to set aside either through savings or a loan $80,000 for your business and a plan of 12 months to start breaking even. If that goal is not met by the end of 12 months, you would need to review all options and seriously consider exiting the business.

Humility over Get Rich Hype: One study purports that 95% of start-ups do not reach their initial income projections and the rate of small business failure in any country is always eye-opening. The business world is a very seductive. You will face many offers that appear too easy or good to be true. "Write a book in a weekend", "secret free website traffic", "flip your first three properties in a month." There is a reason this book is littered with fantasy gifts. There are no magic pills. Follow your key passion at a sustainable rate and speed. The truth is, quality takes time and time requires humility.

Your reputation is crucial and you need to decide whether you are a maker or a marketer first. A pure marketer is solely interested in the bottom line and will flood the market with rubbish. A maker wants to create something of true value, but this cannot be achieved in a weekend. It may take years of diligent effort. I call this "pride over paycheck."

Accountability: Measures like the ones previously provided are required for life and business. Aim to find a positive and supportive confidant and/or group. It is important to be part of two kinds of groups, one being related to business goals and another being related to other interests. The people you are with must be honest and open to exploring their successes and failures and fears. I call it the "No Bravado" policy. Obtaining a mentor that values both business and lifestyle balance is also a viable option.

Passion Focus: Follow your main business passion solely until you have reached a level of success you are satisfied with before branching off into other opportunities. Also, do your best to complete your biggest key business task each day. We are living in a world of full of distractions and it is much more satisfying to fully complete at least one key task than having made incomplete progress with several tasks. Outsource as many non-enriching tasks as possible, so you can focus on what is most essential.

Praise Yourself, Others and the World: Praise is psychological oxygen. Without it, we suffocate under our own fears and doubts. Review techniques in the book for key praise strategies for yourself and others. Gratitude practice is how we learn to praise the world. If there is one simple happiness practice that will give you the biggest result versus the couple of minutes of time spent, it is to write down a minimum of 3 things each day that you are grateful for. This will train you to realize that no matter how difficult the day, there are still great things to be aware and appreciative of.

An additional component is to rate yourself on the effort and not the success you had that day. Effort leads to satisfaction, which leads to happiness, and happiness is the key to success. *To assist you, I've developed a particular gratitude process you can access on the resources page.*

Inspiration Triggers : Inspiration is the greatest form of motivation. Surround yourself with inspiration triggers: music, posters, quotes, people, photographs, meaningful and/or beautiful objects, and the stories of key role-models. This will help you connect to your deeper vision and purpose and encourage you to go for more. That is why in the next section of the book, I briefly mention the inspiring characteristics of some amazing history changing role-models for you to learn about and add to by creating your own list. *I will add a resource in the bonuses to assist you to create your own history defining role-models list.*

Negative Emotion and Commentary Acceptance and Transformation: Your mind and the people in your life generally want to protect you. You will have negative thoughts and fears and the key is to seek the lessons from those experiences. Always ask, "what is this thought or emotion trying to protect me from, and what is the best way to move through it?" People around you will not always be positive either. Some may be very critical.

It is important to respect and consider all "valid" opinions. Ignore or remove yourself from all invalid opinion makers. Inspiration without analysis before implementation can lead to catastrophic decision making. Entrepreneurs tend to want to say "yes", which is why it is good to strategically spend some time with people who tend to say "no." Seek to understand the reasoning behind the critical opinions of others, because sometimes they are right and you will need to adjust your strategy.

Empowering Belief Generation: Developing empowering beliefs leads to optimism, which is the biggest predictor of life success. Your beliefs about yourself and your success, or lack of success, will constantly be challenged. Limiting beliefs around 'being good enough', worthiness, failure, embarrassment, lack of time and resources, self-sabotage, risk tolerance and loneliness all need to be challenged and reframed. *I added a special article to help you through those issues in the bonus materials.*

Stress Management: Well over 50% of workers suffer from significant daily distress (stress management actually refers to reducing distress as opposed to eustress which arises from being in a positive mindset when challenged by activities you enjoy. The exercises in this book are designed to create eustress). Business owners tend to have it even worse. Falling into depression and anxiety and a cycle of fear, failure and doubt, along with obsessiveness are very real risks that every entrepreneur faces. Schedule (di)stress reduction activities in your daily plan. Find at least 5 minutes a day up to three times a day for total silence. This allows the mind to recharge without distraction. The addition of mindfulness practice during silent time *(I'll add an exercise to the bonuses)* can also be beneficial. Go outside for short walks and get some sunshine for breaks if you can, and aim to maintain good sleep patterns, physical health, and nutrition.

Self-Worth must always be greater than Net-Worth: You are more than your business. The other key areas of your life are just as important as your business and make up who you really are. Your goals need to include family, friends, health, hobbies, greater purpose, societal contribution and so on. There are many factors that go into business success and into personal success and they are not always related.

In my opinion, aside from essential quality time with partners, family and friends, everyone needs a creative pursuit (e.g. photography, art, writing, woodwork, music, theatre, restoring objects) and a sport (preferably one done in a group). These are two other areas of life that stimulate psychological growth and add energy and variety into your life. Although you may only be able to set aside a small amount of time for these activities, the return on your self-worth is not to be underestimated. Finding a way to regularly contribute back to society in perhaps small but meaningful ways, has also been shown to boost self-worth.

History Defining Decisions

As you come towards the end of this book and the start of the next stage in your journey, it is important to realize that your decisions - the choices you make to act on just one of your great ideas - may do more than just change your life. They could change history itself! This book has concentrated on entrepreneurship, but really, making that decision to step through fear and into freedom is the universal law of success in any endeavor.

The greatest success comes from those with true conviction behind their decision. Such people are willing to go far beyond ordinary expectations in order to create a truly inspiring legacy. Below you will find a short list of the historic figures that I have drawn strength from. I wish for you too to obtain and utilize all of the qualities listed and more as you progress. I also encourage you to add your own historic inspirations.

On the road ahead, may you discover and apply:

The leadership strength of Queen Elizabeth I, who knew if she was ever to succumb to public expectation and marry, her kingdom would collapse.

The artistic desire of Ludwig van Beethoven, the composer who refused to give into the tragic irony of becoming deaf and producing his best work in his later life.

The patience of Samuel Johnson, willing to spend nine years on the creation of the first major dictionary.

The resilience of Rosa Parks, whose simple refusal to give up her bus seat in a time of segregation became an important symbol of modern civil rights.

The world-changing self-belief of Galileo Galilei, willing to publicly defend and publish a book on his expansion of Copernicanism (being that the Earth revolves around the sun and not vice versa) and being imprisoned for life because of it.

The discipline of Gandhi, whose ingenuity in forming non-violent protest is un-paralleled.

The gentle doggedness of Florence Nightingale, the nurse revolutionist who transformed military hospitals and the mortality rates within them, personally attending to almost every patient despite the initially extreme disapproval of the doctors around her.

The serendipitous ability to find incredible opportunity in failure like Alexander Fleming who discovered the anti-bacterial potential of penicillin whilst aiming to grow bacteria.

The assurance of Walt Disney who learnt to champion his creations from that of a little mouse called "Mickey" to that of an entire theme park.

The self-developmental, business and philanthropic awareness and forward thinking mindset of Andrew Carnegie, who said the first third of life should be spent getting as much education you can, the second third on making as much money as possible and the final third on giving the money away to worthwhile causes.

And to round out the 11 Honorary History Defining Decision makers: May you have the purpose-finding ability of Viktor Frankl in order to overcome and transform tragedy, failure or suffering by searching for the deeper meaning and empowering lessons inside all of your experiences.

In times of doubt, feel free to draw inspiration from any and all the appropriate people that have come before you, and even the positive people around you, whether they are in business or not. Creativity and human achievement transcends category. With that being said, it is now time to start or enhance your passion-based business and put everything you have discovered into action.

Marvels to Mavens: Step by Step
Entrepreneurship from Scratch

The MARVELS model was introduced to outline the skills to develop. Now that you have been exposed to them, the biggest question a budding new entrepreneur will ask is: how do I begin? There is a massive risk of being overwhelmed by the depth and breadth of what lies ahead of you. To answer this question, you need a process to develop the two core aspects of entrepreneurship, or any endeavor for that matter.

The first is your own psychology (your beliefs and habits), and the second is strategies (actual business techniques and procedures you implement). What drives success is the alignment of these two elements. To assist you, a step by step blueprint is offered here, based on everything you have discovered to get you started.

Disclaimer: *The following process is by no means the only way to begin or enhance your current entrepreneurial journey. It is one of many possible frameworks you could draw from. It is offered as a systematic guide based on what you have already discovered to provoke clarity of thought and to instigate a plan of action. By all means, if you wish to follow it closely, then do so. However, no model, no matter how well developed, can ever guarantee your success. Use it as a guide and adjust accordingly based on your own individual circumstances.*

The model to come offers a step-by-step passions-based business blueprint outlined in five phases. If you have already done some of the exercises, simply implement the results at the appropriate point in the process and continue.

As an additional option, I have also added key exercises and talking points to review from the expert interviews. All key talking points and exercises in interview transcripts are bolded for ease of reference.

Phase One: Preparation – Developing the right psychology. This stage is about developing mental clarity and becoming excited about the journey ahead.

1. **Pursuing Passions Exercise (Chapter 7)** – There is no point in embarking on such a massive and frustrating journey unless you first have a clear idea of what you are passionate about, and you have specifically scheduled some fun into your life. This exercise is to help you build indirect business and lifestyle inspiration and ensure variety of activity as you progress.

2. **Develop Deeper Values and Greater Abundance Focus Procedure (Chapter 4)** – Next: You specifically address who you are and the kind of person you are willing to become. This stage is about developing an open and empowering mindset.

3. **Exploring and Setting the Stages of Life Exercise (Chapter 12)** – Before diving into the work ahead, it is important to reflect and take lessons from key life moments up to this point and more importantly, enjoy some of the projected rewards you are to experience in the future. Take special note of the stage you are in now.

Additional Expert Interviewee Tips – Complete Tony Alessandra's obituary writing exercise (Chapter 7) if you really want to work towards an inspiring legacy. If your ideal business is to have pro-social and community building values, review Jenn Lim's (Chapter 4) discussion of their ICEE model and the rules behind their 10 core values. Finally, consider Andrew Griffiths (Chapter 12) advice on how to avoid procrastination and the best mindset to be in when starting a large new project, such as writing a book.

Phase Two: Proceeding – Initial activity engagement. Essential business model creation and entrepreneurial attitudinal skills are now set.

1. **The Mental Preparation for Time Efficiency Process (Chapter 8)** – Moving ahead, focused time utilization and simple goal setting is crucial. Practice this first on a few non-entrepreneurial tasks and then get ready to live and breathe the process once you begin...

2. **Finding the Right Training and Building a Business Model around Your Passions Process (Chapter 9)** - Use this to coordinate your core business planning and training efforts. This is where additional learning in best business practices, advertising, marketing and networking should be done if required. When deciding on your plan, it is easiest if your business has some key unique elements but is still modelled in a legally acceptable way, on a successful business that already exists.

3. **Change Your Future Exercise (Chapter 10)** – This is to develop a well-rounded perspective of the potential rewards and challenges ahead. Do this exercise just before the last step from the above process, which is deciding what courses or programs to do. You need to be sure you can handle the worst case scenario before proceeding with the business idea. If not, you will need to choose a different passion and/or business model. Then complete points 2 and 3 of this section again.

Additional Expert Interviewee Tips – As Eve Adamson stresses (Chapter 9), make sure before you form any consulting type business that you have the training behind you, or are willing to get it. Her other two keys for new venture success are also mentioned in her interview. Adding to this, Tom Butler-Bowdon expresses (Chapter 10) it is important to find a way to enjoy what you are doing every day and to avoid the pitfall expectation of instant success by working to understand "the 10 year rule."

Phase Three: Progressing – Instigating key motivational and momentum building systems.

1. **4 Ps of A-level Accountability (Chapter 13)** – Now that you are beginning or modifying your business, you must demonstrate a daily commitment to progress. Ensure you have frequent contact with at least one other accountability partner and regularly report at every level of accountability. Regular social media and other public declarations of efforts are recommended.

2. **The Positive Appraisal Process [self and/or partner focused] (Chapter 6)** – This process is written to be used with others, but can be easily modified to use on oneself, or be given to an accountability partner to use on each other. Implement in order to maintain and enhance motivation and improve business systems and personal skills.

Additional Expert Interviewee Tips – John G. Miller (Chapter 13) puts it very simply. The core of sustainable motivation is to have a true belief in the importance of what you are promoting and to be accountable to that belief. As you continue to develop your business practices, it is essential as Marshall Goldsmith (Chapter 6) says, to treat all ideas as gifts and minimalize criticism and judgement. He outlines the principles of feedfoward in order to demonstrate effective methods for developing skills and maintaining positive motivation.

Phase Four: Producing – Finding and impressing the right clients.

1. **The 4Cs of Persuasive Communication (Chapter 4)** – Time to begin finding and influencing potential clients. Use the networks and contacts established when you built your business model and utilize the 4Cs to ensure the creation of a professional and persuasive impression.

2. **Snap Judgements Review and Creation Process (Chapter 11)** – After each encounter with potential clients, use this exercise to consider whether they are suitable to do business with.

Additional Expert Interviewee Tips – There are many avenues for obtaining clients. The simplest and most direct method for getting your business off the ground quickly and finding suitable clients is demonstrated by Steve Chandler's (Chapter 8) principles of non-linear time management. Once you have made contact with a potential client, consider using Stuart Diamond's (Chapter 5) three key rules of negotiation.

Phase Five: Proliferation – Expanding the business by modifying or increasing products and services and employing staff.

1. **Creativity Cross-Training Exercise** – Use this to infuse new ideas for improvements in existing products and services, and to assist with the creation of new ones. Ensure expansive changes are ones that you feel passionate about, and that you know you have the competence and time for. If not, do not implement unless you plan to outsource them or to hire relevant staff.

2. **To outsource or hire staff utilize –**
    Snap Judgements Review and Creation Process (Chapter 11) - For finding appropriate people.
    The 4Cs of Persuasive Communication (Chapter 4) – Use the principles of this technique to offer clear, decisive and if required, motivating instruction.
    The Positive Appraisal Process (Chapter 6) – To effectively review their work and increase their confidence and skills.

Additional Expert Interviewee Tips – Consider Randy Komisar's (Chapter 14) advice on how to capitalize on different opportunities by exploring and challenging different parts of yourself in order to grow your potential. Review Richard Koch's (Chapter 11) best new business practices ideologies in order to expand your current business and to enjoy his principles for attracting and hiring superior workers.

Decision Time - Bonus 1

Congratulations for making it through all the Destiny Defining Decisions interviews. My sincere expectation is that you will use their stories and techniques offered as inspiration and fuel for forging your own unique and successful path.

As a reward, I am going to give you a special, unadvertised download link where you can obtain all the radio shows (with all their additional material) on which this book is based. Although the shows are publicly available, I may decide to remove them at any time. However, they will always remain available to you as a purchaser of this book on this private web page link (**FulfillingHappiness.com/dddbonuses**).

As an additional bonus, I also want to offer you one more interview. The bonus interview to follow is quite different from the rest. It was actually created as part of a different project and is actually the first interview I ever conducted. It is also by far my favorite.

I have decided to include it for a number of reasons. The main reason is to show you that no matter what struggles you may face, a positive and inspirational path is possible. The man you are about to meet is not a business or self-development author, and yet I was in awe of his tenacity and his wisdom. He is one of those people where circumstance forced him to make several not just "life changing" but "life maintaining" decisions.

It is also significantly longer than the other interviews, which will allow you to truly understand his mindset and learn from his incredible story. Finally, as another gift, I am going to offer the recorded interview on the private web page link if you want to listen to it at a later time and get a true feel for this man, his message, and what transpired between us.

Enjoy!

To Your New Destiny,

Aleks George

Bonus 2: Back From The Dead -
Special Interview with Anthony Catalano

Aleks: Hi, this is Aleks George Srbinoski from **FulfillingHappiness.com** and welcome to another edition of Positive People. Today I'm talking to Anthony Catalano, author of *I Prescribe A Positive Vibe*. All the information you need about Anthony can be found on his **Facebook** page. Now, Anthony is an incredible example of strength of the human spirit and someone who, despite a very heavy setback, continues to live life to the fullest. So first of all, Anthony, are you there?

Anthony: I sure am, Aleks, and thank you for having us.

Aleks: Okay, not a problem. Great to hear you! Now Anthony, the first question I have is actually why do you prescribe a positive vibe?

Anthony: The main thing for that theme, Aleks, is when I look at the newspapers, the television and actually when I'm out and about and I see a lot of folks that do not have joy. You can just see these people are just walking shells, and they don't realize all the gifts that are around them, all the gifts that are provided for them, and they just don't know how to gravitate to these things. And they just go through their daily lives really not appreciating everything that they really have, and to me it's a very big sadness to see this across the board, Aleks.

Aleks: Okay, so you're saying people cannot see what you see. What is it that you see?

Anthony: What I see, Aleks, is a chance to enjoy every day with quality of living, laughter, being appreciative, love your family, your friends, your surroundings, and really become a person who has their own individuality, but still is not afraid to accept things, experiment in a positive light. **If you don't put yourself in positions to see things in a clearer way, in a better way, you're going to bring negativity into your mind.** And it's just like, I use this as an example Aleks ...

It's like going to a gas station and if you put bad gas into you, your vehicle is not going to run right. It's the same thing for the mind process. If you do not think with a happy heart, a good spirit, and a positive light for yourself and for others, you're going to be a very depressed person, you're not going to have joy, you're going to rob yourself of happiness, and the people around you are going to feel this. So, if you're going to be a shining light for yourself, it will rub off for everybody you come into contact with, and that's the place you really want to be, because negativity will bring negativity. Positiveness will bring a glow, and it'll be a better way to show yourself, and it just elevates everything around you.

Life is too short, Aleks. When you're 20 years old you think one way. You're 30, you think another way. And we all go through a process along the way. We learn things, and hopefully we cultivate wisdom and knowledge and a better understanding that the ride of life is very quick. You've really got to grab it, run with it, and absorb the blows if they do come.

Now, a lot of people don't want to hear such things Aleks. "Oh, it was raining today, I couldn't go to the beach" or "Oh, I missed an appointment" and things that are very trivial. If you let those type of things get in the way, yes, they might be an inconvenience, but if it rains, God needed to water his land. You know, things of that nature, there's a hundred things you still can do to bring light to your day. So, it's not always looking at the dark, you've got to find that light, no matter what it is.

Aleks: I think we can allude to something here. I guess you could say you're uniquely qualified to be able to prescribe that kind of mindset of making the most from each day. Why is that?

Anthony: Well, back in 1985, I was engaged at the time. We were going to get married in June of '86. Life was great, healthy, strong, vibrant, young, and the whole world was at our disposal, and all the stepping stones to a future were right in place.

And on this fateful Monday morning, a cold, dreary day, my fiancé tells me in the morning, "Don't go to work today" and I said, "Honey, I gotta go to work." It wasn't like she had a premonition of anything, but I said, "I've gotta go in" and I went.
And subsequently, Aleks, after lunch I was one of the first construction workers back on our site, and we needed an air tank from one of the buildings we were working on. And just like a normal thing to do, I would climb up the elevator shaft. I looked around, and the cement was already being poured. So plan B is you have to walk across the braces to get to the other side.

Upon doing so, the first step I took, and there's nothing to grab onto, Aleks, I went down into the elevator shaft, I hit the floor below, I went to get up and I rolled through the hole again. Boom, I hit again. Still was a little winded, but I felt okay, and as I went to get up one more time, I went through the hole again. And boom, when I landed a third time three stories down, I'm looking up at the sky and I'm just numb. And I'm telling myself, "What did I do, break my arms, my legs?"

I didn't fathom that I just became a quadriplegic and severed my spinal cord, and I didn't feel any initial pain or discomfort of any sort. And I heard the guy high up saying, "One of your guys is down, one of your guys is down!" And of course, they stabilized me and actually took me across the street to a metropolitan hospital, which was on 96th Street between Second and Third Avenue in New York City, New York of course.

So, upon this all going on they're cutting my clothes off and putting heat on the back of my neck and I'm like, "What is actually going on?" I'm telling myself. And then my fiancée came and I said, "Ah, I'll be fine, I'll be fine" and low and behold I wound up getting a collapsed lung, getting pneumonia that same night, and they rushed me to Bellevue Hospital, Aleks, and upon there I almost passed because my breathing started to fail.

So, they needed to perform a tracheoscopy for me. So, now I'm on ventilator and my thoughts are just racing a mile a minute, "What is going on?" and we really weren't getting clear-cut answers for a couple of days. Things were just starting to feel very strange in my body, and my mind started play havoc on me like, "Wow, this must be something very serious."

And low and behold, Aleks, I found out, "You've severed your spinal cord. C4 was crushed, C5 was severed. Welcome to a new world, a new way of living and this is what's ahead of you now."
So, just like that, Aleks. No really – how can I say? No pre-warning, nothing to prepare for. It was just an incident that – boom, things do happen that quick.

I was a very big, strong-type guy. And I've seen things happen to football players and athletes and other people in walks of life. You just never think it's going to knock at your door and when it does, it definitely is a wakeup call to "this is real now, what are we going to do from here?"

Aleks: Yeah, now I mean that's just incredible. So, at one moment you've pretty much obviously got all your faculties, you're loving life, you're eager, you're young, you're free spirited, and then you've got this incredible crushing or spirit crushing – at least in the first instance – event where everything changes. And I'm just wondering, those first few days when these things started to become real to you, what was that like for you?

Anthony: Initially I was in intensive care for 44 days and I was very warm, my temperature was always warm, and I had to drink and I really couldn't speak. And when the doctors were actually making the rounds I was actually forcing myself, "Am I gonna live, am I gonna live?" And then obviously they weren't going to answer me, but they circled me and this went on twice a day.

My fiancé came and friends came and family, and I just tried to still maintain a sense of "I'll be okay. I'm gonna be okay." **I was always a very competitive guy, Aleks, and I think that really was part of the equation to keep me focused, keep me alive because I had a defining moment, and I'll allude to that when we get to it.**

But, at the time my fiancé was a very big support to me. She was there through it, through all that process and God bless her and thank her for every day of my life. But, it came to while these days were passing and finding out what actually is going to be, and the mountain now that I had to climb in such a different way. It's either you're going to grab this thing and not only make a life for yourself, but a quality of life.

I didn't want to be a sad story – "Ah, the poor guy" and wind up in a nursing home or even worse, Aleks, I've seen big guys in rehab. I've done some motivational speaking and I've seen some men and women crying, just their spirit is crushed, they just don't have the fight, the fire, the desire to see past this and just know this is fate.

I mean, **I went through the process "Why me, how could this happen to me?" Of course, it's just natural human instinct to go through this. But after I got through all that process it was "Why not me? I can do this. I'll be a soldier for many others and I will carry the torch." And I can say I've been blessed with good people around me, Aleks, to help me when I needed.**

But, **I mean the desire had to come from within. If you don't push yourself no matter what your walk of life is, it doesn't have to be from a catastrophic injury, it needs to happen across the board.** When you wake up, wake up happy, wake up smiling, wake up with joy, wake up going out your door and seeing the flowers, the ocean, the trees, the beaches, your family, your friends. These are the things that are important, these are the things that are real, and these are the things that should be everlasting.

We're all going to have sadness and things are going to come to each and every one of us, it's inevitable, but through this journey, Aleks, I scream as loudly to all the listeners and the people that have listened to me and have followed *The Positive Vibe* that this is something you need to incorporate every single day. Live this way, you'll enjoy yourself and your life so much more.

I mean, I can bicker and I can complain, oh, you know the simplest things, Aleks, like getting up out of bed to get a glass of water or turning on the tele is a far-gone memory for me now. It's just like "Wow, my mind still thinks just like it did before the injury, but the body is not reacting." It's there, but it's just not happening. So the war now is within yourself, your mind and thank God I've been pretty much a strong, confrontational type of person.

A lot of people say, "Oh yeah, you're able to do it but not everybody's made that way." Well, you've got to find what works for you, but if you start thinking negative no matter what it is, you're going to feed yourself bad and pretty soon you're going to be consumed with it. Ah yes, my walk [laughs] in life, no pun, is definitely a very tough thing to do.

My wife of almost 17 years now always said, "Anthony, **you were a big strong man before the injury, thank God.**" **But the true test of any individual, Aleks, she tells me is the inner strength. That's what will catapult you to a life of happiness no matter what comes. I mean, I had things easier in certain ways, Aleks, but I do what I got to do, I get past that, the rest of the day, the evening is as good as anybody's on this planet.** I make sure of it for myself and everybody around me.

When you look at Anthony in the chair, Aleks, you don't see a poor guy in the chair "Oh, this that." You see Anthony, you see the smile, you see the glow, you see the life that you can tell is there. And that is the art of anything to maintain, you've gotta find that feeling inside of you and just hold it every day and let it shine.

Aleks: I think that's brilliant, Anthony. There's so much to learn just in that, just in those few minutes that you just spoke of, and what I find interesting about you is there's a juxtaposition between this really tough, New Yorker, with the Italian-American accent. We see it all the time in the movies, which is just, it's kind of great to actually speak to someone who kind of sounds that way, which is really cool.

So you have this obviously tough, driven person, but at the same time I've seen the joy and the sweetness and the softness in you, as well. I've looked at some of your poetry, and it's so not expected from someone from your background. Can you tell me a little bit about how you merged the two, the strength that you have, this sort of the classic strength versus that appreciation of life and that softness that comes with it as well?

Anthony: Aleks, very perceptive in that last comment. I have a big smile on my face because yes, I do have that New York bravado, but I've always been the type of guy even as a kid, Aleks … I come from a very modest family, with just my mum and dad and myself and we lived in a very modest six-family apartment. And no, none of the niceties of what maybe a lot of the other children had, but I can say I had a very loving growing up situation.

So, when I was out and about even at 12, 13 I remember quite vividly if I saw an old man or an old lady crossing the street and struggling with a part of their groceries, I wouldn't even think twice of going over if I knew them or not and say, "Ma'am, sir, can I help you cross?" And gladly would do that, you know, "Do you need help with your laundry?" It was just the nature I had. I was a big, strong guy, but I never would bring that in a negative way. And sports, I was very good at a lot of sports, Aleks. I didn't have that chip on my shoulder, what I did was my work and that was enough for me.

And when you talk about, I'm like the gentle guy from New York and you read some of the poetry, and you see the sensitive side I do have. I'm a very, how can I say, well how to say it in that way … I'm a very loving type of man, that I'm a humanitarian. I love the animals, I love nature, I love people that really do things in a positive light and try to help one another.

There's so much ugliness, across the board, the news what they force feed on us, all the negativity. I mean you become numb anymore to any of this stuff, I mean I almost don't want to watch it, I mean it's just like, "Ah, six people killed or this or that" and all of a sudden it's just a couple of different names and in three days, two days you forget who they were and you get the same stuff coming back at you.

So, I'm trying to really get the word out there. Let people get on the right side of the fence and not be pulled into this muck and this turmoil and this tailspin that society across the board is really headed for. And, a lot of the children today, **the values aren't the same as when I was a kid. A lot of things they expect these days. That work ethic and taking pride in what you do and what you gain for yourself is a lost art, and I think we really need to get back to these type of things or else everything is really going to be a big problem as we go forward in this world.**

Aleks: Yeah, look, I think you're very, very perceptive. I mean, in my line of work I usually find the science and the statistics behind a lot of the observations you've made. And yeah, I mean they've done studies where there really are many, many more altruistic and positive acts that occur in a day than negative acts, and yet you'd never see that on the news.

And I think that's the news really working on the fear principle, which is basically as humans we react first and foremost to fear and to stress and that sort of thing, and so it pulls people in to watch. But yeah, over time it really just sort of sucks away your strength and your perceptions of people in general. I mean, if you're constantly looking at "Oh, this person killed this person and this person robbed this person" and all these things which obviously do occur, but it's not an accurate view of the world and of how our society can be.

Anthony: And that's the sad thing. It's a travesty, Aleks, and that's the damage that the news, the media is doing. They're stereotyping people all across the board, they're making people look down and frown upon others and they know what that does, you get categorized, and now you're just in a group, and this is what you are and this is what you are when that's the furthest thing from the truth.

I've got friends in all walks of life, all races, colors, backgrounds, and they're some of the most beautiful people in the world. But, when you get classified as something and people who aren't open minded and are just tunnel-visioned into the negativity and force-fed into their heads. Wow, you're causing a problem, you're causing a gap, you're causing division. Where's the unity, where's the love, where's the respect for each other? You know, we're all different in certain ways. That's okay. **I don't mind you being different, but if you're a good soul, you're a good person, and you're doing the right thing, that's the winning combination there.**

And that's what we all need to put aside, we talk about this here and there, Aleks, and even in my country here I'm disappointed at certain things. Oh, the government and the things that go on and then they try to, the B.P. incident we had here, and what a shame, I mean it's just these things. Yes, accidents do happen, but these things shouldn't happen with the technology, the smarts, the engineering. It hurts me.

I see things happen in other countries, it hurts me. All of the stuff in the Middle East and whatever else troubles are it's amazing we can't band together we all look for this power and control. It's just going to erupt, it's going to blow up and there's not going to be a return.

I mean people have just got to turn away from that sight of what they're being fed and find their niche, find themselves and just be a good soul, to be a good husband, be a good father, a good son, a good friend. This is the quality, don't be deceiving, don't be lying, don't be negative. And I'll tell you, when we used to watch the shows, Aleks, I'm almost 50 years old, and I remember watching the shows like *Leave It To Beaver* or *My Three Sons* and *Family*. When all those shows were coming on it was a simpler time, but there was a lot more balance in those days.

Now you've got all these reality shows, all these far-out things going on. We've become a society of acceptance, which is fine to a degree, but you're letting it run wild, out of control, no boundaries. Now, look what you've caused.

Aleks: I guess what you're talking about there is setting a standard, a standard of behavior, a standard of thinking, a standard of morals, and I think that's obviously something you live by and something you have to live by to make the most of the life you have now since your accident. And it really is a shame that people aren't being challenged to live to a higher standard.

And you kind of remind me of ... I think many children have this desire to be the hero, and I'm pretty sure you had that desire in many ways as a child and even in small acts when you help a lady across the street there's that little bit of that feeling of goodness, of something pure, of something genuine and caring and loving.

And, I can see that's something that comes out in you, this sort of this desire to, it doesn't matter if you're in a chair or not, this desire to make that positive impact on the people you meet and in a bigger context as well with the people you haven't even met through your book and your interviews and other sources.

So I really do commend you for that attitude that you have and the way you've presented yourself so far. What I'd like to know now is just tell me a little bit about a day for you, because obviously there must be many challenges in just a normal day for you.

Anthony: Aleks, I will tell you this. I don't sleep much. I wake up probably at 5:30 in the morning 7 days a week, **but when my eyes open up, Aleks, I'm electric. I don't yawn, I don't like, "Ah, give me another half hour, another hour." My eyes open, the day is here, let's get this show rolling.**

I have a friend of mine who's actually like a brother now, comes in, he's been with me about 16 years now. And he's just like family now. We have a routine we have to do, I have to get up, I shower, I shave, go to the bathroom, I brush my teeth and do all the necessities that anybody anywhere else has to do. I'll get back in bed, I'll do my range of motion. I'm still very healthy, very strong.

I will share something with you, Aleks, along this topic. And once I get back in I'll actually start writing. I'm on Facebook, and I actually write every day. And my wife thinks it's a funny thing that I could watch let's say a scary movie and all of a sudden I'm writing this beautiful, romantic piece and she looks at me like, "How do you come up with this after watching a movie like that or if we're having dinner and all of a sudden you come out with these things?"

And I really have no set pattern or answer. I could just say it's just like wow, I just get this kind of like a tap on the shoulder. I put a line or two on paper and all of a sudden it just comes to me and I share it. It could be about love, romance, politics, Jesus, a life, the flowers, the ocean, rain and I'm very broad spectrum in my writing and thinking, which I think is a very good attribute, because I've got so many different people that like this type of writing, like that and it's like "What is he going to write this morning, what is going to write this afternoon?"

And I've got so many beautiful letters and comments and e-mails of what I've done for people. I've got to share this with you, Aleks, two things that really moved me and that stayed with me and will stay with me forever. When I started writing, oh probably about nine months ago, I was just getting through four surgeries on my bottom. It just wasn't healing, I almost passed away in December of '08. What happened was a decubitus ulcer happened, and I went to a place here in Florida and they really weren't the best and it got worse, so on and so forth.

And I had a lot of problems, I almost spent 9 months out of 12 stuck in bed and I had friends call me saying, "Anthony, why don't you get on Facebook and connect with some of the friends and help pass the time sort of thing." So you can imagine, Aleks, being paralyzed is one thing. I can live the lifestyle of being in the chair pretty easily. **My wife says, "You know, you remind me of a guy on a float. You wave, you're happy, you're always smiling." And I said, "Baby, this is just the way it's gotta be you know. It's gotta happen every day. Not every day I feel the best, but I'm gonna bring the best." And that's what I expect every individual to do.**

So, through that process, Aleks, of being stuck in bed and the clock was my biggest enemy. I'm turning left to right, right to left, that was my day. Eating in bed, going to the bathroom in bed. Just a very trying time, but still finding ... "This is going to get better, I'm going to get better, I will be better and then everything's going to be just fine." So, I don't take medication for my mind. **Everything is done within me! I digest a situation no matter how big, how small it is, I look left, I look right, I look ahead of me and I look behind me. I see the possibilities and then where the light is, that's what I shoot for.**

And it could be a small light; I knew I was going to be stuck in bed for months. Wow, you're talking about really dealing with a traumatizing situation. What had happened, Aleks, since that I had to re-acclimatize my body to getting back up consistently again, getting my blood pressure back in sync. **I mean I go through so many things behind the scenes that people can't even imagine on a daily basis, but I do it, I do it diligently, I do it routinely, and I get through it.**

I've got a system that's pretty much flawless and I live that way in my life, and I take care of my father-in-law who lives with me the last two years, my folks who are up there in the years. I've got no blood brothers or sisters, so basically everybody leans on me still. So, I don't mind it, I'll carry it as much as I can, Aleks. I feel it's my duty, it's my honor, it's a privilege to still be here, and anybody I meet or talk to I don't judge. If you're a good soul and you're a good person and I get a good vibe from you, you're going to get the same in return. And if you're having troubles, I'm going to try to help you unravel some of them troubles and maybe not have them tomorrow, or next week, or next month, and that's the whole key.

So, once I get back in bed and I do my range [of motion] and I do my little writing in the morning, I'll get up for the day and boom, what does it entail? Well, I do a lot of writing still. Book two is done, it should be coming out in about 45 days. I've got enough material to do books three and four right now, so I plan on the *Positive Vibe* to be a five-book series, which I plan or hope to do in maybe within two or three years I'll be finished and complete and out there. And that's what I want to happen, if I can make a difference, Aleks in a hundred, a thousand, ten thousand households, I've done my job.

Aleks: Oh, I think you're making a difference every day just in the way you conduct yourself, and I think that in itself has a ripple effect. So, to actually have a book out, that is also a wonderful addition to what you're doing and a great way to do it. I guess we all want to be remembered for something, hopefully positive, and it sounds to me that's very much the direction you've taken. You really can't take life for granted with your condition.

Sometimes these challenges come up which you mentioned, being in the chair, being in bed for 9 months which is just really, really hard to imagine for so many people. And yet you're there, you're writing every day, you're focused, you have a mission, and I think that's really important, this sense of purpose, this mission you have. How would you define your mission?

Anthony: I feel that every day that I wake up, whether I was in a chair or not, but being in the chair now that it's another opportunity to save someone, to wake somebody up, to get somebody on the right track, to let them see it's not as bad as you're really thinking, you've got to look at things in another light. You've got to grab it this way or you're slowly going to suck yourself dry of every good thing that you do probably have around you, inside you. And that's the chaos I see in so many people.

I can go shopping, I can go to a ball game, I can go to a concert, Aleks, and you just see people just with those dull looks and attitudes and you just wonder why. You see them walking with children and families and they just, they just look like there's a loss, they're just *there*.

So, **my plight is every day do what I got to do for me, and people didn't realize when I was writing, that I was writing bedside with the side of a pinky, because being a quad, my hands don't open and close, so my writing when I'm in bed is being done with a side of a pinky. And my book that I just wrote was done in three months once I started to get rolling.**

I always was a guy that had a lot of family and friends, and if they had questions or concerns they would come to me and I would give them the one on one "Rah, rah" my perspective, my ideas, how to maybe approach it, and I've helped many that way, but now with the book I hope to reach so many and now the second book where I've been back in my lifestyle, I've got my health a hundred percent again. I'm up and around.

I've driven to New York three times in my custom van. I go to car shows; I get a lot of joy out of that. **I've created a van with a lot of art work and the lights and a lot of bling going on in there. It's a fun thing because when I go to the shows, you're interacting with people and not only is the van a super van, but they're seeing a fella out there in my situation who is alive! He's bright, he's happy, he's enjoying! And it just elevates people who don't have my situation.**

A funny thing, Aleks, a lot of people on my Facebook … are you are familiar with Facebook I'm sure?

Aleks: (Jokingly) Yeah, we're not that far under a rock over here.

Anthony: No, I didn't think so! (Laughing) I didn't think so, but you know how you have the profile picture. Some people show this or that and most people. I've got a picture of me usually of just seeing my smiling face. So, unless you really know me, you don't know that I'm sitting in a chair and living this lifestyle. So people when they peruse through my photos, they see me, my family, friends, they'll see pictures of me when I was up and around and not injured at the time, and then they'll see the process that I share with them.

You know "Oh wow, this guy's had something happen. Wow, he's in a chair. Wow, this guy writes like this, he's got a wonderful, loving heart, Wow."

And all that type of thing really opens their mind and their eyes even further, because there's not one day I will write on Facebook or anywhere about me being in a chair, that my day "Oh, I had to do this today. Oh, I had an accident. Oh." You know, things of that nature. I just put my helmet on every day, what will be will be, and I'm going to make it the best it's going to be.

(Part 1 End in Audio, Part 2 Below)

Aleks: I think what's really amazing about you so far, that from when I've known you, is one thing I really believe in is you lead by example, and I think that's your motto. You have to lead by example really, you don't have a choice, but that's the key really to happiness and to helping others.

You can have all the great advice, but unless you live by that advice, unless you really, unless people can feel that this person is congruent, that this person is genuine, authentic in what he's saying and what he believes and can inspire people through that, it's just not going to work. And there's so many people that tell you what to do, but they don't live what to do.

They don't show you what to do and it sounds to me like that's really something that runs through you, this desire to live and to live by what you say and to be the completely congruent person that you are where's it like "This is me, this is who I am. This is how I see life and if I can see life this way, and live this way, then so can you."

Anthony: And that's the theme, and that's the truth and that is the bottom line for all of us, and that's why in a world that we all reside in and we see everything going on around us ... We all go in our little homes, and we'll discuss day's events, and we'll talk around dinner and we'll discuss this, that and the other and "What's the issues and what's the problems and what's going on?"

But, if we all could be one voice in one big house and really, really listen to each other, then I think we'd have the gold we need, because you turn on that television and you see that going on. Ah, it's just the element that doesn't get us beyond.

You know, over here for us, taking away "I pledge allegiance," not allowing that in the schools and maybe to say a prayer in the morning for the children. You know you create a mindset that way, you create a goodness, a genuine good feel. If you don't do these things you see kids running amok, and the behaviors are getting worse and they're out of control and a parent especially if it's a single parent now you know the respect factor and just the continuous tailspin that this causes, because when you create this environment like this one leads to another to a domino effect.

It just keeps stirring and how much more can you put into a box or into a bag before ... and that's what I see going on in a big way so we got to be soldiers, to really get out there and we got to get these powerful words out there, the positiveness, the goodness. **It's an individual fight right now, everybody's all about themselves instead of the teamwork, team is what makes you win. If you don't have a winning team, you got a few weak links in there, you're not going to be the champion you need to be so you need to get a team together that is pulling the same way, thinking the same way and ultimately going to win it. Totally, every day. So, you've got to be surrounded with this.**

Aleks: Obviously you're speaking of a winning team which obviously leads to one question I have for you, is this I'm sure incredible partner of yours. So you're going to have to tell me a little bit about her.

Anthony: My Linda, my Linda Rose, and I'm smiling. When I went through my first separation with Donna at the time, that is the period where we left New York back in August of '87. Reason being the accessibility, the weather and for me being in my stomping grounds and when I was up and around was pretty tough for me to digest on the daily ... because when I first got out of the rehab and everything I was in an electric chair that looked like a monster machine, and I had these splints on and I could barely move then and I was in this electric chair and I just felt very down, very blah. The eyes were on - theirs were on me then, "Oh, poor Tony" or "Poor Anthony" and it did bug me at the time knowing that "Wow, this is where I'm at. This is what's going on." And of course all the body changes, the mind wasn't where it is today.

So anyway, we decided let's go to Florida because of the ability, the life change it'll give us a breath of fresh air and the sunshine, of course. Well, lo and behold, Aleks, we came down here, we rented a place and then we bought a place around the corner and we had a very loving relationship. It's a shame because at the time we were young and we were together before I got hurt and I was always a take-charge type of guy and I did a lot of the things for us. And now the roles were totally reversed, and the things that she had to do for me not many could do for their loved one, and she did it like a champion and willingly and lovingly, but it still wasn't enough for me at the time to see past it because I still didn't know what is Anthony going to become. Am I just going to be like this?

And slowly but surely we fell apart. I kind of pushed her away because I kind of shut down at that period. It wasn't that we stopped loving each other. I mean we would cry in each other's arms for four hours in bed knowing that this is it, you got to go your way, I've got to go mine. And we did and the tough thing then like I mentioned earlier I had no brothers or sisters. I'm in Florida, I know a couple of people but Anthony's basically alone, what do you do now?

So, Aleks **I had a *defining moment really*. It was either I make this work, I make this life happen or I'm going to be done. So I found a few people finally and it took me a while to get people that really cared about Anthony, his plight, and his desire to live and that were reliable. Some of the people they sent me from nursing agencies and what not, I couldn't sleep at night and couldn't trust and had to weed all that out until I found my team, so to speak.**

So once I had the team, I would go to Tampa General, which was an hour ride, three days a week. Started to get myself created again and what I mean by that is, I've got to do more than I'm doing now. So I've learned how to do a lot more things for myself to get my independence. I was the first quadriplegic to pass the driving class at Tampa General when they started it.

Aleks: Ah, well done.

Anthony: What an accomplishment that is because I'm in control of not only me, but the people riding with me and the people on the road. And that was something that I'd take a lot of joy in every day I hit the streets. Upon that, I went back to school, finished my high school, graduated, went to college. Took some classes, took some accounting, went to a tech school. So now, slowly but surely my stepping stones of getting Anthony to a new life, a new lifestyle, and a better living situation was starting to come.

Now Linda, my wife of almost 17 years, was one of the first nurses that came my way and she's also a fellow New Yorker. She is from Long Island, I was more from Queens near the city. And as soon as we got together we kind of hit it off as two people, and there was just a nice thing that bounced off of each other. And we didn't date initially at all; I mean she just was one of the nurses.

The funny thing was, when I was going back to get my high school taken care of, I met a girl there. And at the same time I was in that electric, I wasn't driving yet and I would be dropped off and picked up. And she found something in me that she liked, but she became very smothering. A wonderful girl, nice girl but I just wasn't ready for that and that was a big thing for me, can I find love again, will I fall in love again?

Let me tell you this, Aleks, by the grace of God **I've never had a problem with females in my life, even after the injury, even though of course the obvious I can't do everything like I used to, but what I can do I guess is pretty darn good, because I've had relationships since the falling out with my first and then when I shut down with that girl Meg, I actually started driving, I started working out more.** My mindset was really getting a kind of head steam, I can be with a female and things are great again.

So, basically other than walking, let's let this thing roll now. And that's what happened, I built myself a home and I moved a little bit away from where I was and then Linda and I kind of ... 'cause I fancied her, but I didn't know how much she liked me, but we didn't know much ... I dated while she's still one of my nurses and had females stay and she would be in the other part of the house.

And I told her one day, I said (jokingly), "You keep putting me out to the wolves, and I'm going to be gone. Well, I'll always be your friend." "Yeah you think so, huh?" (her reply).

Well, we had a defining moment and lo and behold we're now come December it'll be 17 years. So, she's a wonderful girl, spunky, spry, full of life, a joy, never complains, and she's a softie, but strong. So, it's a good balance, it's a good blend, and we're both very fortunate for each other.

Aleks: And I think it's amazing because one thing I always say is that emotions are contagious and emotions are the key to attractiveness. And I think that's that part of you, that you're saying you never had too much trouble with women, I think that's because of your personality; because of the emotion you're presenting which is out of, despite your circumstances still confident, still loving life, still fun, still I'm quite sure humorous.

All these kind of key characteristics that are just so attractive to anyone and people, they don't see the chair, they see you and that's what you present, and I think that's so incredibly refreshing to hear. I love the fact that you're saying that these women would be attracted to me despite your circumstances, because it really is, that's the key to attractiveness. How you present yourself, what you're giving to others, the kind of emotion you're presenting.

Anthony: And that's actually been a gift, and I take a lot of joy from that. Even when I'm on Facebook and a lot of the people that have read my writings and they actually can feel the individual that I am on a daily basis. They come to the page and see I'm continuous, it's not like I'm there one day and I'm not in three or four, I'm there in the deep seven days a week no matter what I've got going on in the rest of my life, I make it a point to be there.

Then, for myself people write to me all the time asking me questions and they've got this going on and that. And I actually take the time and I use this as an example. Let's say if you're a musician and you're in a band and you're on stage and your fans are there and they're, they're loving you and they're pulling at you, you got to play and you got to be there and let them know you love them too.

And it's the same thing with my writing. If you're not there, you kind of lose the trail, you lose the heat of each other and I love the people that respond to me.

I mean they're great friends of 40 years ago or they're great friends and people I love from three months ago and it's an instant kind of connection that you'll know.

Like, I'm from New York City and I've been exposed to that learning that really you can't get in any school. I've seen the best and the worst there, and really my Dad was a great teacher. He actually drove a taxi in New York City for 40 years and he took me downtown, midtown, uptown when I was a very young guy seeing Times Square when things were really crazy, and just trying to let me be aware of the elements and what is out there. You know we're in a nice little area, where things were nice, a nice little neighborhood. He exposed me as a teaching, and I really absorbed it so whenever I was in those elements, I kind of knew how to adapt to circumstance and I think that was phenomenal tool for me, even though this is a major, major thing that I go through all the time.

Vacations are great, but unless it's accessible they're more of a pain in the butt than anything. I've really got to find my spots and I think that is the blessing that I do have joy, I do love what I do, I do love where I'm at right now and what I'm doing for others. I just feel like I'm just like one of God's soldiers that **this was my fate, this is what was meant to be, you can't moan about it, you can't change it, you can only grow from it and that's what I want to share with the listeners, the people I come in contact with. No matter what you're doing, where you are in your life, make it happy, make it better.**

Enjoy what you do, enjoy what you don't do. And just grab that theme, and you'll see a quality of life just be a breath of fresh air. Always see the rainbow, never see the turmoil of what's out there. **It's like a door, if you go left maybe you're going to find one incident, you go right you're going to find another. So you've got to pre-program yourself for what you've got to be doing. If you've got to work today, be glad you're going to work, be glad you've got that job, do your best while you're there. Know that after the job is done, you go home, you eat, you relax, you unwind, and you do what you do. And then you enjoy that phase of it.**

Everything is a cycle. You sleep, you wake up, you do this, you do that. Some people got to do things one way, some go to do the other. And another thing that I think is very important for the listeners, and I say this and I want them to really understand. Money is a great accomplishment in the world. When you look at the big business moguls, you look at the high profile athletes, you look at actresses and actors. **The money is a nice convenience, to know I don't have to have worries about my bills this and that, but does that really guarantee any of them inner peace, an inner core of happiness?**

Well, I tell anybody "no," because how many have we lost along the way that have had all that money comfort, and for one reason or another got caught up in a situation or surrounded themselves with people that took them down, and lo and behold they're gone. All the money in the world, it didn't mean nothing. It didn't change nothing. So, you need to change you first before anything. So, whatever does come your way, you appreciate it. If you get all of that kind of monetary status, then you learn how to handle that. That's just like handling anything. Your emotions today, how you're feeling, what you're going to do and how you're going to do it.

So these are lessons that money doesn't work when you hear people, "Oh, if I had money I'd be like that ..." No, it doesn't work that way.

Aleks: Yeah, I don't think it's the money, I think it's if you had a mindset like this, you'd be like that. If you had a mindset like this, you'd be that way. I've studied the whole relationship between money and happiness, and you're absolutely correct. Money does not guarantee happiness. In fact, often it can go the other way, and I think money's very important. It's a very useful tool. Obviously you'd know about this, to take care of your bills and so forth, if you had a bit more money that would probably help.

But it can't be the key of why you're alive. It can't be the key or the main focus of your day. I think as humans we're here to build relationships, and that's the main focus of why we are what we are and why we do what we do. And so statistically, they've done the studies and money does not guarantee happiness, it really doesn't.

It's a useful tool if you have it, but the key, it has to be something deeper, something that helps you connect with other people and I think that's what you're basically saying, what's coming through you right now is this idea that people have money and they're still miserable. Well that's because they have a mindset of misery. The money is just the tool or a tool, there's many tools. And the mindset is really the key, and I think that's where your great strength is coming from.

Anthony: And you're so correct when you say those words, Aleks. The mindset and it all goes back to square one. We start out as a child and we find our way, and we kind of cultivate and learn who we are and what we're capable of. We have engineers, we have politicians, we have waiters, we have chefs, we have people that do sanitation, or police officers. Nobody is any better than the next person. Some people might be in positions that we would earn more that way.

But I got to tell you this, no matter how much you make, you're not going to take a nickel of it when you go to the next phase of where we go from here. What you're going to take with you hopefully is a pure, good heart and a good soul and a good spirit. And that you want to take with you every day, because that's real, that's guts, that's blood, that's strength there. So, people listening out there, you need to get yourself together, have a positive outlook, a positive mindset and a positive being.

You put these into your mind and digest it as the gas to fuel you every day. No matter if something doesn't go your way or not, it doesn't matter. It will pass like a cloudy day. **You just got to keep plugging, keep pushing, keep believing and living this way. And you'll see before long while you are cultivating yourself in this frame of thinking, everything will be better around you. The flowers will look prettier, the sky will look more beautiful, the waves will be more stunning to you, the mountains will be breathtaking to you. This is the way you got to go.**

Aleks: Sure. I think unfortunately many people unlearn the natural joy that comes from it. I guess that's why I do what I do, to help people re-learn how to love life, experience life, and to succeed in the way that's meaningful to them. I think if I was to break up some of your mentality just quickly … I talk a lot about mindfulness and what mindfulness is, it's just basically awareness. Awareness of what's around you and being able to appreciate, being able to be grateful for what's around you.

And I can see that's something that obviously you cherish each day. This great perception of all this incredible beauty and nature and just inspiration around you, and you've sharpened your mind to be able to capture that and even to write about that.

Anthony: And that's the thing, Aleks. People, they leave their door and they ignore the beauty that is right there in front of them. The flowers, the trees, nature, the animals, the life that is provided for us. And this has all been created for our joy and pleasure, but if you go out there thinking with these thoughts of "Ah, I got to go to work. Ah, I got to do this. Ah, I can't believe I got to do that." Wow, you're headed for a dead end. That wall is going to come quickly in, your doors are going to be narrowed and your mind is going to be narrowed and your life is going to suffer for it.

So, listen to Aleks, listen to Anthony out there and grab on to these positive thoughts and lifestyle ways of being. For your own sanity, your own being, you need to incorporate this immediately. You can't think about this you can't **"Well, I don't know and I don't know if I can do it." Yes you can, yes you will, yes you are. There's no turning back. Losing is not an option and it's not in the equation. No. So, get a grip, see where you are, see what is ahead of you. Turn off what was behind you and start going forward, whether you crawl or you run. Go forward, you must.**

This is where every individual has this opportunity to do this. It's not for some people and not for others. This is for everyone. This is global happening right now. So, grab on to the positive, let go of the negative and you'll be a better person for it. For yourself and everybody around you. There's no way that this won't happen.

Aleks: I think that's brilliant, and I can feel, and like I said I always talk about feeling, because basically as humans that's what we want. We want to feel. I can feel this determination come through you whenever you speak about your kind of natural life's purpose and daily purpose. Where is this determination coming from?

Anthony: Aleks, I tell you I get to the juice from, I guess coming through that period where I almost passed away. You know living, I'm almost 25 years as a quadriplegic, and through those 25 years I really didn't have any wound issues, only when I first got hurt because they didn't really take care of me and cure me properly when I was in the hospital and what not.

But once I was home, I was fine. But still, Aleks, as those years were going through, I was enjoying life, I was doing fine and I was helping as much as I could along the way, but **I'll tell you the truth and it might sound strange to some people but I'm almost glad that I went through that period where I was stuck in bed. It really defined how valuable life is to me, it really let me express and find the writing that was always inside of me, but I didn't put it to utilization until my back was against the wall.**

There's another thing, Aleks, I got to share. Those are the two things that I almost forgot. About six months ago, there was a 16-year-old beautiful girl from London. Her name was Chloe Maria. I'll never forget these two things I'll mention with you, three things. And all of a sudden, and back then I really wasn't as how can I say astute, or maybe clever or precise in my writings as I became. But the message obviously hit her directly and that to me was golden.

She got on my page one day and I almost can quote her as saying, "You've changed my life. You've changed my whole life. You're a master craftsman of words. I would buy your work. You should become a poet." In big bold letters and I'm looking at this and I'm like, I took a step back in my chair and said, **"Wow, if I can reach a 16-year-old girl in London who's going through her changes, her life, and whatever else is going through her at this time, and I'm making an impact on her like that. Wow, I'm doing something, Anthony. You're really, you're connecting, you're making a difference."**

Then a great girlfriend of mine bought one of our books, and she shared it with a great friend of ours and at this time, it wasn't too long before that her mom and sister were tragically killed in an automobile accident. Well, when she read my book, she wrote to me in big, bold letters about five different times already that, "Tony, if it wasn't for your book, I don't know how I would have gotten through some of my days and nights.

I feel like you wrote this book for me and I'm so thankful for your wisdom, your courage, and just your heartfelt expression in your words."

So those type of things, Aleks, I get all the time from people that have read the book or have read my writings daily and the other thing I want to share that really woke me up. A few years back I was in a supermarket and I was waiting for Linda to grab a cart. And lo and behold you're looking around to see what's going on. And I looked and I took another look, and I took another look, and I see I'm sure you know the push carts, you can put your groceries in, and you can put maybe a baby sitting in the front there and you can put their legs through …

Aleks: Sure.

Anthony: Okay, I'm looking and I see this gentleman pushing the cart and on each side of the cart holding the cart with like a six-year-old girl there and like an eight-year-old girl, I guess his daughters. And I looked in the cart and what I thought was maybe a third child, my eyes just got so wide and I got chills instantly. It was his wife whose arms and legs were cut off at the joints totally. She was a head and a torso basically, sitting there and the rest of the supermarket is just going by like nothing.

To me, I looked up at the sky, I thanked the good old Lord Jesus. I said, "Lord, I am so blessed. I am so blessed." And that has left an impact on me, that really has, I get choked up when I visualize that, every time I talk about it. That really was a defining moment to me, you need to get this out there. You need to let them see. You need to do this. You're in a good position to do this.

And when **I saw that poor woman, Aleks, I could only imagine. I mean, she couldn't even have scratched her nose, or feed herself or anything. It was just, it was really something for me to see. It definitely woke me up in a big way of understanding where I am. Yes, I have a lot to go through, there's no lie to that, but I'm thankful that I can get through it, and I'm thankful that I'm still moving forward.**

I'm almost 50 Aleks, but I'm told I look like I'm 37. That's another good thing. I don't eat fast food. I don't drink, and I don't smoke anymore. So that is another few things that people need to take awareness of. Don't put poisons and toxins in your body, and don't eat crap foods with preservatives and all those hormonal things.

As long as there's a bunch of people in the world, these big conglomerates, these big store foods, they don't care if you get sick or ill. That's why they got hospitals and if you pass there's always another one. I feel like we're sheep and they're the shepherds so to speak. So you got to careful that way, too.

Aleks: I see, you've got to become your own shepherd.

Anthony: Ah ha, there you go. Yeah, but I'll tell you, I'm going to make sure my sheep are okay.

Aleks: [laughs] Very good. Very good. All right, I just want to let you know we're coming to a close here. I just want to ask a few quick questions. Just simple off the top of your head answers. What is happiness to you?

Anthony: Happiness to me is getting up and knowing that I have another opportunity to think good and to reach another person. To me that really is a goal that I try and strive for every day when I write and if I get responses from people that haven't responded that much or "Wow, I love this" or "Wow, did you write this for me?" And then they know because I expand on responses and I try to keep a log if they liked what I wrote there, I will copy, paste and put it in kind of storage so then it might be utilized in another future writing or in another book.

And then the joy of just my family's okay, my immediate friends and everything is okay and we're able to go out and enjoy the day. I'm a simple type of guy, it don't take much to keep me happy. I don't need the material things, that doesn't move me. It's just the people, I'm all about people.

And I just want this whole society to maybe just go back, take a step back, look around and challenge yourself for the positive. Don't grab that tailspin. It just happens to often, Aleks. I can't say enough about it. You'll hear me beat that drum until I get it through their heads.

So, yeah that's what moves Anthony. **Meeting people, helping them and letting them see me for who I am, the way I am and if I can do this, I really want you to try to do it for you. There's no reason you can't. There really isn't. The only thing that's going to stop you is yourself, and that's your mind, your physical-ness. That is the only thing for you to get from point A to point B. Don't point fingers. Don't boo hoo. Don't moan.**

Grab whatever you got to grab. Put it in your pockets, put it in your mind and get there. Do it. You might need to do a little work, it might get a little difficult, but do it, please. For your own self.

Aleks: Well, you know what. I have to say I've learned so much from you. This is what I really love about interviewing people, especially someone like yourself. You know I've been to school, I've got a whole bunch of degrees, I know all these different facts and sciences, but you've got the real qualification, which is life, and you're someone who without a doubt has said, "Okay, this is what life has given me and this is my response." And it's been such an incredible, empowering response and it's been just such a pleasure to hear from you, to speak to you, to learn from you, like I said because everyone has a story to tell, everyone has lessons to give, and you are very qualified to be a speaker about happiness, to be a speaker about making the most out of life, success, you know you really are because you've lived it and you keep living it and I can't wait to hear more about you and to look at the new books and that sort of thing. I think it's just going to be absolutely brilliant.

Anthony: Aleks, I have to tell you. The instant vibe, we are not around the corner from each other and for you to have found me, and to have read and had the interest, I want to thank you first and foremost for inviting us and taking the opportunity to share this with each other. I consider you a good friend, and I hope this isn't the last time we talk, so you'll have to include a number where I can reach you and reach out from time to time to say hello.

And last but not least, if I may, you can find us on Amazon.com, Borders.com, BarnesandNoble.com *I Prescribe A Positive Vibe* or to do a name search for me on **Facebook.com**.

Aleks, also, one last thing I want to leave with and the lesson is, if you're going to be the light, you need to bring yourself to shine every day. **You need to be the shine in the sun so to speak. Because if you bring your A game every day, whoever's around you has no excuse but to bring their best with you. And if you float and you act a little weak or a little off, you're going to allow room for others around you to do it also.**

So, even though you're not feeling your best, you've still got to bring that element that you're going to give your best. It may not be the best song of the day, but at least you're going to sing. And then that's the theme for people to understand. I have my own interpretation of trying to elevate people's minds and character and well-being so hopefully my words and my honest love for people that I don't even know, Aleks. And when I give them like the same love of somebody I've known 40 years, I'm true to myself and I'm true to what I believe and fight for. And in your country, I hope your world is beautiful, and I hope your family and friends are all okay, and I wish this across the board.

Aleks: Well look, it's been an absolute pleasure. And like I said, you really are someone who is really qualified to talk about these topics, and I really love that about you, and I've learned so much from you and I absolutely can't even comprehend how much I've learned from you. I'm just going to have to listen to this interview again and really dissect some of the things you've said and really continue to use them to help others.

And it's just been absolutely brilliant, so I want to thank you so much for your time. It's been absolutely wonderful, and I definitely will be keeping in touch, so thank you very much, Anthony.

Anthony: Thank you so much, Aleks and I wish you nothing but the best, my friend.

Congratulations

Thank you for reading Destiny Defining Decisions. My objective with this book is for your experience to feel like a coaching session where you spend minimal time reading and the majority of your time applying. If you enjoyed it, I would appreciate your support.

Please take a moment to leave a review of this book on Amazon. I value your feedback and it helps me to write about what people want.

Help me to help you by helping me to help you with your review :)

http://www.amazon.com/Aleks-Srbinoski/e/B005JWGWWY/

Use the above link to offer a review and view my latest books which are listed below. The first two listed (**) are also available in print.

- Maximum Mental Health: Overcome Depression, Anxiety and other Mental Illnesses with 20 Principles for Happier and Healthier Living **

- Happiness Up Stress Down: Increase Happiness and Decrease Stress in just 2 Minutes a Day over 2 Weeks and Help your Community **

- Motivation Now: Productivity and Persuasion Secrets for Modern Day Excellence and Effectiveness

- Instant Inner Calm: Simple Stress Management Strategies to Increase Clarity, Creativity and Calm

- Precision Language: Powerful and Precise Positive Thinking Secrets for Personal and Professional Success

- The 7 Mental Viruses Crushing Your Potential: Overcome Fear and Negative Thinking by Building a New Positive Mindset

- 10 Life Success Secrets Revealed: Your Simple Guide to Success, Wealth and Fulfilling Happiness

For mass copies or training, email: aleks@fulfillinghappiness.com

Final Call – The FREE Extra Resources Page

It is your final call. If you have enjoyed the journey, don't let it end. Keep the momentum!

Right Now - Jump onto the free extra resources page. Or if you have downloaded them, jump into those resources and get going.

I want you to really start flying by giving you:

- **All 11 radio show/seminars on which this book is based**
- Bonus Interviews
- **A High Level Goal Setting Process**
- Cheat Sheets and Templates
- **Fast and focused self-development techniques**
- And More…

Take off the right way by going to:
FulfillingHappiness.com/dddbonuses